Driving Growth

About the series

The McKinsey Global Institute (MGI) was established in 1990 as an independent economics think tank within McKinsey & Company, the management consultancy, to conduct original research on critical economic issues. Its primary purpose is to provide insights and facts about developments in the global economy that will help business leaders and policymakers to make better decisions.

This anthology of articles published by MGI is part of a multi-volume set. Each volume presents conclusions drawn from MGI's principal research projects, in particular over the past five years, illuminating related themes.

The Productivity Imperative: Wealth and Poverty in the Global Economy

Articles in this volume show why and how the level of productivity in an economy—the ratio of output to input—is the key determinant of its rate of growth. In studies of numerous economies around the world, both developed and emerging, MGI has measured productivity levels sector by sector and analysed how they might be improved.

Driving Growth: Breaking Down
Barriers to Global Prosperity

This series book describes three barriers to productivity improvement that MGI has frequently encountered in its studies on productivity in individual countries.

Offshoring: Understanding
the Emerging Global Labor Market

This volume in this series of anthologies contains articles that estimate the likely extent of offshoring and how businesses and policymakers on both sides of this emerging global labor market can better manage the phenomenon. The key is not to obstruct offshoring, but instead to make sure that some of the resulting gains are directed towards those who lose out from it.

Driving Growth

Breaking Down Barriers
to Global Prosperity

Edited by Diana Farrell,
McKinsey Global Institute

Harvard Business School Press
Boston, Massachusetts

Copyright 2006 **McKinsey & Company, Inc. United States.**

All rights reserved

Printed in the United States of America

10 09 08 07 06   5 4 3 2 1

No part of this publication may be reproduced, stored in or introduced into a retrieval system, or transmitted, in any form, or by any means (electronic, mechanical, photocopying, recording, or otherwise), without the prior per-mission of the publisher. Requests for permission should be directed to permissions@hbsp.harvard.edu, or mailed to Permissions, Harvard Busi-ness School Publishing, 60 Harvard Way, Boston, Massachusetts 02163.

ISBN 10: 1-4221-1009-5
ISBN 13: 978-1-4221-1009-6
Library of Congress Cataloging-in-Publication Data is forthcoming.

The paper used in this publication meets the minimum requirements of the American National Standard for Information Sciences—Permanence of Paper for Printed Library Materials, ANSI Z39.48-1992.

Contents

The key to growth: breaking down barriers to global prosperity

Economists generally agree that the foolproof method for increasing a nation's income is to improve productivity in every sector of the economy. There is much less consensus, however, on how best to improve productivity.

In the course of the McKinsey Global Institute's research on economies around the world, we frequently encounter three beliefs about productivity growth that evidence from our studies does not support. The first misconception is that a direct correlation exists between investment in information technology and productivity; this is the myth of the so-called "new economy." The second holds that productivity in service industries—especially local services, such as retailing, accountancy and electricity supply—is of minor importance in countries seeking rapid GDP growth when compared with performance in manufacturing or high tech. The third belief is that, in any particular country, the extent of the informal economy, made up of enterprises that evade taxes and ignore most business regulations, has little or no impact on productivity and growth in the modern, formal economy.

These three misconceptions have important consequences for policy. Their persistence among development economists and policymakers leads them to advocate strategies that can hinder rather than enhance productivity growth, in some cases seriously. They constitute barriers to greater global prosperity that have been widely overlooked.

This anthology collects the 10 articles by MGI that we believe best demonstrate the case against each misconception. The collection also presents guidelines for policies regarding these three areas that will raise productivity more reliably, by promoting investment focused on productive innovation, encouraging greater competition and growth within service sectors, and by effectively and fairly curbing the informal economy.

The articles are arranged in three sections.

1. IT spending and productivity growth: the real relationship

Two contradictory views on information technology and productivity gained credence in the United States in the late 1990s. Before the dotcom bust, it seemed to observers that unprecedented investment in new technology could have moved the US economy onto a permanently higher plane of productivity growth. However, after the slump in technology stocks in 2000 and the ensuing economic slowdown, many company leaders concluded that excessive IT spending was the root of all their problems and squeezed IT investment to a trickle. To get at the truth, MGI examined the relationship between labor productivity and IT spending and use in 20 industries in the United States and Europe in the five years to 2000. That research, described in this anthology in "The *real* new economy," showed that productivity had only forged ahead in those sectors experiencing intense competition. This prompted managers to innovate, often using IT. However, companies in less competitive sectors that also invested heavily in IT, such as retail banking, saw little or no productivity improvement.

The research makes clear that IT investment alone does not automatically result in higher productivity from the firms making the investment. "Getting IT spending right this time" shows how companies can refine their IT investment to be more certain of productivity gains. Investments that apply carefully sequenced IT-based improvements to the key levers affecting productivity in their particular industry are much more likely to yield productivity improvements. Accompanied by complementary adjustments in management processes, this kind of targeted IT investment can yield durable competitive advantage to individual firms.

A deeper understanding of the real relationship between investment to promote innovation and growth in labor productivity is particularly relevant to Europe's leaders today. Faced with chronically low average productivity growth across the region, and increasing competition in many traded sectors from lower wage economies, policymakers in the EU are searching for policy solutions. Generally boosting state and corporate investment in research and development is a popular candidate. However, "A road map for European economic reform" shows that, while first-class R&D will be important to Europe's future growth, removing the barriers that still obstruct competition in several European sectors should be the policy priority. The article draws on MGI research on productivity growth in Europe's major economies to show that stimulating competition will spur firms to innovate faster, resulting in the kind of focused, high-return R&D spending that Europe's leaders need to promote.

2. The impact of productivity in services on growth

Over the past half century, a range of strategies have been adopted in emerging markets to promote import substitution, export manufacturing, and, more recently, services for export. Policymakers have created fiscal and regulatory regimes biased in favor of the strategy adopted in their country. But in doing so, they have consistently underestimated the contribution to GDP growth that can be made by improving productivity in domestic, as opposed to traded, services. These range in scale and influence from consumer services such as hairdressing, and business services like law and accountancy, to the services based on physical networks, such as telecommunications and electricity supply, which underpin a modern economy. "Domestic services: The hidden key to growth" explains the importance of services to GDP and employment in all economies as technology change in industry reduces employment in manufacturing, and advocates an approach to regulation that will boost service productivity.

Governments provide a wide range of domestic services, often on a huge scale. For instance, the UK's state-owned health service provider, with more than 1.2 million staff, is the largest single employer in Europe. But as people live longer, and their expectations rise, funding pressure on government services, such as pensions and health care, is growing the world over. Raising productivity in government services is one way to lessen the pain of the coming budget crunch this will produce in many countries. "Boosting government productivity" draws on the experience of governments in more than 50 countries to show how this exceedingly difficult challenge can be tackled.

In countries like Mexico, where recent growth has indeed been fueled by export manufacturing, the emergence of competition from countries with even lower labor costs, China in particular, can seem a paralyzing threat to policymakers. But "Beyond cheap labor: lessons for developing economies" shows such fears are exaggerated. As countries become wealthier in a globalizing world, their economic policy must of course adapt to changes in their relative production costs. Providing higher value-adding services, such as design and marketing, is an attractive option for economies that have so far relied on providing cheap labor for foreign manufacturers. Jobs in these areas are much less likely to switch location in response to small changes in relative costs than manufacturing jobs requiring less differentiated skills. Losing low-wage, low-skill jobs to China is therefore not a setback, but positive proof of a country's progress up the economic ladder.

Competition from imports made in lower wage economies has also been widely blamed for the continued decline in manufacturing jobs in the United States. "Don't blame trade for US job losses" shows that the truth is much more complicated. In the United States, as in all countries, manufacturing employment declines over time, due to changes in technology. Even China, the "world's factory floor," shed 15 million net jobs in manufacturing between 1995 and 2002. In the United States, it wasn't rising imports that continued to destroy most manufacturing jobs after the end of the last recession, so much as falling exports. Their decline was in part a result of the dollar's strength over the period, fanned by the growing budget deficit and other countries' currency management regimes. So protecting the economy against imports would fail to reverse the job decline. Moreover, it would risk damaging the United States' large and growing trade surplus in services, an important source of new jobs for the US economy. The real but harder-to-implement solutions are to stimulate domestic demand, cut the budget deficit, and persuade countries with artificially cheap currencies to let them appreciate against the dollar.

3. How the informal economy stifles competition in emerging markets

Not only do many policymakers and development econo-mists believe that a large gray economy, comprising unlicensed activities by unregistered businesses paying little or no tax, is ir-relevant to a country's overall economic growth; some also argue that a burgeoning informal sector is a blessing for coun-tries experiencing rapid rural-urban migration, because it will create jobs much faster than the formal economy can. But MGI's country studies show that quite the opposite is true: large informal economies seriously distort competition, and thus re-strict growth in both output and employment. "The hidden dan-gers of the informal economy" explains how the gray market in any sector unfairly tilts the playing field. Because informal enter-prises gain a large but unearned cost advantage by evading tax and ignoring regulations, they make it almost impossible for for-mal competitors to grow market share through improvements in productivity. But if productivity among modern, formal players does not improve, employment and growth in the formal econ-omy as a whole are restricted. This article sets out a policy framework that will curb the informal economy effectively and fairly, thus accelerating growth and employment in the economy as a whole.

"Reining in Brazil's informal economy" and "The cost of the gray market in Turkey" provide detailed case studies of the consequences for two emerging markets of permitting their gray economies to flourish. The informal sector in both puts a powerful brake on the rate of growth, locking them into an "emerging but never quite making it" state, and condemning those living and working in the gray economy to a lifetime of insecurity and poor living standards. Their experience demonstrates that curbing informal activity should be an urgent priority for policymakers in developing and emerging markets pursuing faster economic growth and higher living standards across the board.

The main forces driving entrepreneurs in countries with large gray economies to operate informally are unreasonably high taxes on business and the bureaucratic burden of conforming to local business regulations. "Regulation that's good for competition" shows that economic regulations contribute most to economic development when they are targeted at facilitating fair competition. Among its recommendations, the article advises regulators to level the playing field by enforcing fair business regulations evenly across the economy. Setting corporate tax rates at a reasonable level, and applying them firmly to every enterprise will signal an end to the kind of permissive culture that encourages government officials to turn a blind eye to informal trading. Several countries taking this approach to regulation have succeeded in bringing informal operators into the formal sector.

—Diana Farrell
Director, McKinsey Global Institute

1

The *real* new economy

Diana Farrell

IDEAS IN BRIEF

Competition and innovation—much more than IT—fueled the productivity surge of the 1990s.

Innovations during that period boosted productivity. As productivity rose, competition intensified, bringing fresh waves of innovation.

The key to success in today's economy is to foster competition in order to spur innovations. These may depend on highly targeted investments in IT, but IT investment alone will not automatically lead to higher productivity and growth.

Amythic aura surrounds the soar and swoon of the "new economy." The scale was breathtaking, illusions abounded, and the forces at work seemed at once powerful and elusive. As the bubble inflated, many felt that information technology, and the Internet in particular, would "change everything." Today, with the technology sector in shreds, more than a few believe that IT changed scarcely anything at all. The truth, of course, lies somewhere in between. But where? What became of all the innovation we thought we were seeing? What actually happened to productivity growth? What effect did IT really have on companies and their ability to compete? Most important, what can managers learn from it all?

For more than two years, the McKinsey Global Institute has been studying labor productivity in the United States, France, and Germany and its connection to corporate IT spending and use. My colleagues and I have examined a large body of statistical and experiential evidence and conducted in-depth case studies of 20 industries, eight in the United States and six apiece in Germany and France. The studies involved not only the collection and analysis of data on industry and company performance but also extensive interviews with executives in each sector.

We found that a new economy did indeed come into being in the 1990s, but that it is very different from the one that was widely promoted and discussed at the time. Rather than springing from the Internet, it emerged from intensifying business competition and a resulting surge in managerial innovation. Information technology's role in the new business world, we also discovered, is more complicated than has been assumed. IT is of great, but not primary, importance to the fate of industries and individual companies. By uncovering the true drivers of corporate success today, our research provides a clearer understanding of the recent upheavals in business and points the way to a more effective deployment of corporate IT investments and assets.

The truth about productivity

Something did change in the economy in the late 1990s, and it is visible in the productivity statistics. After growing at an anemic 1.4 percent annual rate from 1973 through 1994, US labor productivity shot up 2.4 percent a year from 1995 through 1999. And productivity has remained fairly vigorous even during the recent economic downturn, rising at 2.9 percent in 2000, 1.1 percent in 2001, and 4.8 percent in 2002, according to the Bureau of Labor Statistics.

The late 1990s productivity surge coincided with a big increase in the money and attention US companies devoted to information technology. In many industries, technology spending doubled as businesses wove computer and communications systems more deeply into the fabric of their operations. Overall, the percentage of the gross domestic product accounted for by technology goods rose sixfold, from 2 percent to 12 percent, during the decade.

Not surprisingly, many people looked at these numbers and concluded that the IT investments drove the productivity gains. But it's not that simple. When we examined the performance of different industries, we saw little correlation between productivity and IT investment. Although most industries significantly boosted their IT spending, their rates of productivity growth varied enormously. In fact, in the United States, productivity gains were concentrated in just six sectors: retailing, securities brokerage, wholesaling, semiconductors, computer assembly, and telecommunications. These sectors account for only 32 percent of the US GDP, but they contributed 76 percent of the country's net productivity gain. Many other sectors, such as hotels and television broadcasting, invested heavily in IT but saw little or no productivity growth (see "America's uneven productivity boom").

If information technology wasn't the primary factor in the productivity surge, what was? The answer is clear: Intensifying competition led to productivity-boosting innovations in the six key sectors. Our research shows that managers in those industries were forced to innovate aggressively to protect their revenues and profits in the face of strong competition. It was those innovations—in products, business practices, and technology—that led to the gains in productivity. In fact, an important dynamic

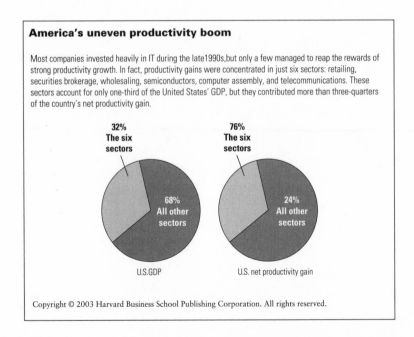

America's uneven productivity boom

Most companies invested heavily in IT during the late1990s,but only a few managed to reap the rewards of strong productivity growth. In fact, productivity gains were concentrated in just six sectors: retailing, securities brokerage, wholesaling, semiconductors, computer assembly, and telecommunications. These sectors account for only one-third of the United States' GDP, but they contributed more than three-quarters of the country's net productivity gain.

32%
The six
sectors

76%
The six
sectors

68%
All other
sectors

24%
All other
sectors

U.S.GDP

U.S. net productivity gain

of the new economy—the *real* new economy—is the virtuous cycle of competition, innovation, and productivity growth. Fierce competition spurs innovation, in both technology and business processes. These innovations spread quickly, improving productivity across the sector. As productivity rises, competition intensifies further, bringing a fresh wave of innovation.

The crucial role played by competition can be seen clearly in the performance variations that were evident across countries and industries. In sectors where competition was promoted— through the dismantling of regulatory constraints, primarily— innovation flourished and productivity soared. But wherever regulation or other forces warped the competitive environment, competitive pressures eased, innovations failed to develop or to spread rapidly, and productivity growth slackened.

Look at the mobile-telecommunications industry. In the United States, the government's auction of additional spectrum in 1995 led to increased competition, with the average number of competitors in a local market jumping from two to almost five. Prices fell, usage increased, and the entire sector's productivity grew at an average annual rate of 15 percent during the decade. That's a very healthy rate, yet it pales in comparison with the 25 percent gains posted by the mobile-telecom sectors in France and Germany. The difference is that US regulations created a fragmented and protected market with dozens of subscale regional providers and little national competition. Today, more than 50 providers serve fewer than 200,000 customers each in the United States. In France and Germany, by contrast, a handful of national providers serve an average of 10 million customers each. The strong rivalry among the big European providers, as well as their superior scale, led to the exceptional productivity gains.

Such differences between nations were evident in other sectors as well. Competition in retail banking, for example, is freer in the United States than in Germany, where small state-owned and cooperative banks have been unable to build sufficient scale yet remain shielded from the shareholder demands of capital markets. Our study showed that weaker competition kept German banking at a significant productivity disadvantage, even though the sector grew healthily as a result of higher customer demand and a wave of consolidations. Retail banking productivity in Germany was only 74 percent of the US level by the end of the 1990s.

In food retailing, France fell behind the United States in productivity gains. Again, the culprit was restrained competition. Zoning laws effectively shielded the dominant French hypermarkets from innovative competitors, and smaller, traditional merchants also enjoyed considerable governmental protection. The productivity of the French grocery sector actually fell at a 0.5 percent annual rate in the 1990s, while US food retailers posted 1.6 percent annual gains.

Competition was not the only force driving productivity in the 1990s. Strong consumer confidence, for example, led customers to purchase more expensive goods, which also helped boost productivity. And buoyant capital markets contributed to gains in the securities sector. But our research clearly shows that wherever competitive intensity was greatest, innovative products and practices proliferated and productivity grew robustly. And wherever competition was constrained, innovation waned and productivity suffered.

The role of information technology

When competition intensifies and companies face the possibility of lost customers and profits, managers have overwhelming incentives to pursue creative ways to cut the costs of their operations and increase the value they provide to buyers. The choice really is to innovate or die. There are many ways for managers to innovate, of course, but during the 1990s information technology proved to be a particularly powerful tool. We found three reasons why that was so. First, IT enabled the development of both attractive new products and efficient new business processes. Second, it facilitated the rapid industrywide diffusion of innovations. And third, it exhibited strong scale economies—its benefits multiplied rapidly as its use expanded.

IT's power to promote innovation was not felt equally in all industries, however. The sectors most dependent on intensive information processing—those with highly complex operating processes, heavy transaction loads, or technically sophisticated products, for example—reaped the lion's share of the gains. When an industry had such characteristics and exhibited intensifying competition, productivity boomed.

New products and processes

Some of the IT-based innovations of the last decade came in the form of new products and services (such as faster microprocessors or on-line securities trading). Others were enhancements to existing business processes (such as check imaging and centralized credit authorization in retail banking). In many cases, the new products and processes were tightly intertwined. In the semiconductor industry, for instance, the rapid increase in the complexity of chip designs required ever stricter process controls and diagnostics. That spurred the development of sophisticated new information systems for managing chip fabrication, which boosted productivity throughout the sector.

The six industries we identified as showing the greatest productivity gains during the 1990s all leveraged new IT capabilities to create products or refine processes. Sophisticated new IT systems were, for example, a godsend for retailing. Big retailers execute millions of relatively small transactions each day, creating extraordinary operating complexity. IT helps them manage that complexity much more effectively. It not only automates routine functions such as inventory receiving and control, price scans, and checkout, it also optimizes many complicated processes, including supply chain management, merchandising, and customer relationship management.

Securities brokerage is another information-intensive industry that benefited greatly from new IT capabilities. Between 3 million and 4 million securities transactions, with an average size of $25,000, take place in the United States each day. With the spread of the Internet, innovators like Charles Schwab and E*Trade were able to incorporate highly efficient on-line trading into their already productive discount brokerage models. Our research reveals that, without on-line interfaces, these brokerages would have needed ten times more brokers or other customer service employees to handle the demand they encountered. The adoption of on-line interfaces has been remarkably swift. Almost no retail brokerage trades were executed on-line in 1995; by 2000, 40 percent were handled over the Internet. Interestingly, on-line trading was the only instance in which the Internet contributed significantly to the economy's overall productivity jump during the so-called dot-com boom.

In US wholesaling, the use of IT in distribution centers significantly boosted productivity. By combining relatively simple hardware (like bar codes, scanners, and picking machines) with sophisticated software (warehouse management systems for inventory control and tracking, for example), wholesalers were able to partially automate the flow of goods and thereby reduce labor costs significantly.

Diffusion

As new technologies spread across a sector, they often had a striking impact on productivity. In the retail sector, for instance, many companies were quick to adopt warehouse management and automation systems, bar code scanners and readers, and ERP modules for human resources, payroll, and reporting. Those systems helped automate processes that traditionally required large staffs, leading to significant reductions in labor costs throughout the industry. In the US trucking industry, major carriers rapidly embraced network optimization systems and bar coding and scanning technologies, driving productivity gains across the sector. French and German trucking firms, only recently exposed to strong competition through EU deregulation, lagged in their adoption of these new technologies. As a result, their productivity remained well below that of US companies, with France at 85 percent and Germany at 83 percent of US levels.

Technological innovations not only increased productivity in some sectors; IT itself also directly facilitated the diffusion of many business and technological innovations. Companies used more sophisticated corporate planning tools, improved communications systems, and continuous on-line monitoring to increase the speed with which they replicated the breakthroughs of their competitors. New technological capabilities played a particularly strong role in spreading innovations across distribution centers and stores in the retail sector and across banking and brokerage branches in the financial sector.

Fast diffusion is a double-edged sword, however. While it improves overall industry productivity, it can erode the competitive advantages of individual companies. Once rivals in a sector adopt an IT innovation, after all, it becomes just another cost of doing business. As a result, many companies that spent heavily on state-of-the-art technology in the 1990s failed to recoup their investments. On-line banking spread so rapidly, for example, that no individual bank was able to reap any competitive advantage—the benefits all went to customers. (In this case, the banks also had unrealistic expectations of changing consumer behavior. US customers have adopted on-line banking so slowly that it has yet to have a major impact on sector productivity.)

The secret to retaining an edge from rapidly diffusing technologies, we found, is to couple them with other distinctive capabilities or processes in ways that are hard to replicate. JP Morgan Chase recently used IT to augment its strengths in the automotive finance market. In early 2001, the financial services giant had 9,000 dealers in its system and was a leader in the prime-lending segment. It then dramatically extended its distribution network—to 18,000 dealers—by rolling out its on-line DealerTrack system, which dealers use to help customers find and close loans electronically. Because DealerTrack supports JP Morgan Chase's existing advantages, its benefits cannot be easily copied by competitors—even if they install the same technology.

Scaling

The benefits of most IT innovations grow dramatically as scale increases. Once you install new software for transaction processing, for example, the marginal cost of processing additional transactions falls rapidly toward zero. Indeed, given the often high upfront costs of adopting a new technology, achieving scale is often crucial to reaping a return on an IT investment.

When technology innovations spread equally through countries, we found their impact on productivity could still vary widely depending on the extent of industry consolidation. IT innovations had their greatest impact in industries with a high degree of concentration or with a high volume output per customer. Retail banking is a good example. Retail banks in all three countries we studied have automated their back offices, enabling them to service a virtually unlimited number of transactions at negligible marginal cost. Yet US banks have enjoyed the greatest productivity gains. That's because US consumers typically carry two to three times more financial assets and loans than their French and German counterparts. US banks simply process more transactions per customer.

German retailing is also illustrative. Weak corporate governance kept unproductive German retailers in business, leading to overcapacity and meager profits. That limited German retailers' ability to invest in the IT-enabled, long-term efficiency improvements that some French and most US retailers were adopting.

A new agenda for IT

Even in the six sectors that gained the most from IT, many companies failed to earn strong returns from their technology investments. Some simply abandoned new systems when implementation difficulties arose or costs exceeded expectations. Others took a piecemeal approach, automating only parts of their business processes. Still others didn't invest in the areas with the biggest potential impact on productivity or invested too early in systems that competitors could easily copy.

Some of these errors seem surprisingly obvious. But in retrospect it's easy to see how some managers in the late 1990s got carried away with IT and spent money unwisely. As IT investment soared, so did productivity growth, economic growth, earnings, and stock market valuations. IT took on the appearance of a panacea, leading many managers to assume that "me-too" investments would pay off.

There's much to be learned from the companies that gained the most from their investments. Our research revealed, in particular, that three practices distinguish the companies that were most successful in their IT investments. First, such companies targeted their investments at the productivity levers that mattered most for their industries and themselves. Second, they carefully thought through the sequence and timing of their investments. Third, they didn't pursue IT in isolation but rather developed managerial innovations in tandem with technological ones. Let's look more closely at how these imperatives drive productivity. (For a discussion of the implications of these imperatives for technology companies, see "The challenge for IT vendors.")

Target the productivity levers that matter

There are many ways to improve productivity, as "Working with the productivity equation" illustrates. You can reduce labor or other factor costs. You can increase labor efficiency or asset utilization. Or you can sell new or higher value-added goods to your customers. IT can play a role in each of these areas. The trick is to concentrate your IT spending on those levers that will have the greatest effect on productivity. Many companies we looked at spent heavily on seemingly attractive new technologies, only to find that they had little effect on results.

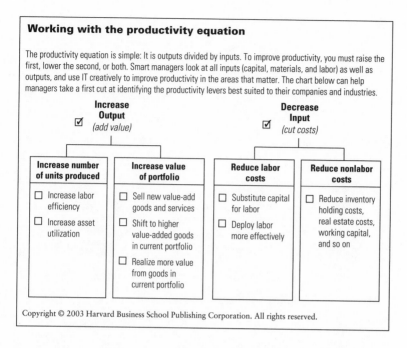

Working with the productivity equation

The productivity equation is simple: It is outputs divided by inputs. To improve productivity, you must raise the first, lower the second, or both. Smart managers look at all inputs (capital, materials, and labor) as well as outputs, and use IT creatively to improve productivity in the areas that matter. The chart below can help managers take a first cut at identifying the productivity levers best suited to their companies and industries.

☑ **Increase Output** (add value)

☑ **Decrease Input** (cut costs)

Increase number of units produced	**Increase value of portfolio**	**Reduce labor costs**	**Reduce nonlabor costs**
☐ Increase labor efficiency ☐ Increase asset utilization	☐ Sell new value-add goods and services ☐ Shift to higher value-added goods in current portfolio ☐ Realize more value from goods in current portfolio	☐ Substitute capital for labor ☐ Deploy labor more effectively	☐ Reduce inventory holding costs, real estate costs, working capital, and so on

The levers that matter vary from industry to industry. That explains why the IT applications with the greatest impact are often tailored to particular sectors. We found, in fact, that no general-purpose application had much effect on productivity. In retail banking, customized applications for automating lending, credit card operations, and back-office transactions provided the greatest boosts to productivity. In consumer retailing, the key applications focused on streamlining distribution and logistics, merchandise planning and management, and store operations. In the semiconductor industry, the greatest gains came from highly specialized tools for electronic design automation, process control, and yield optimization. CRM applications, on the other hand, generally purposed to increase revenue through better customer management, tended to yield mostly poor results.

Even within an industry, different productivity levers can have very different impacts. Consider retailing. General merchandise retailers like Wal-Mart are low-margin, high-turnover businesses selling a vast number of items, many of which are consumer staples. They get the most benefit from tools such as warehouse and transportation management systems that allow for a tighter link with suppliers and an increase in inventory turns for a given product. On the other hand, specialty-apparel retailers like the Gap handle many items with short shelf lives and therefore rely on assortment and allocation planning tools to cut obsolescence and inventory-holding costs. Among electronics retailers like Circuit City or Best Buy, store allocation and price optimization tools play a key role in reducing markdowns. Home improvement retailers, whose profits hinge on after-sales services such as warranties, home deliveries, and repairs rely on extended order management systems to ensure greater customer satisfaction.

As these examples show, simply following broad IT trends can backfire. The smartest companies analyze their economics carefully and spend aggressively on only those IT applications that will deliver outsized productivity gains. As for other necessary applications, they seek out the cheapest possible solutions. And they always remember that the system that pays off for one competitor may do little for another. Take supply chain management systems, for instance. Spending on these popular technologies has proven to be a boon to general merchandisers, but comparable investments by apparel companies have yielded very little.

Get the sequencing and timing right

IT investments build on one another, often in complex ways. Companies that install sophisticated (and expensive) new applications before they've done the necessary groundwork are almost always disappointed. They either fail to achieve the expected benefits, or they find themselves doing constant retrofitting. But companies that take a disciplined approach, sequencing their investments carefully, often reap great rewards.

Wal-Mart's "step change" approach to IT investment during the 1990s is a great example. First, the company installed software to manage the flow and storage of products through its far-flung network of suppliers, warehouses, and distribution centers. Once it had automated product flow, it focused on using IT to coordinate its operations more tightly with those of its suppliers, leveraging its greater efficiency. With that smoother coordination, Wal-Mart could invest effectively in technology to plan the mix and replenishment of its goods. Finally, after integrating all these capabilities, the company built a data warehouse that uses information pulled from a range of sources to handle complex queries.

Kmart, by contrast, made a misstep in its IT investments that undermined their effectiveness. It invested in systems to improve promotions management before it had installed the supply chain systems necessary to handle fluctuations in sales volume. As a result, it was unable to capitalize on the more precisely targeted promotions. Many retail banks also made errors in sequencing. They invested in popular customer relationship management systems before they had built repositories of consistent and reliable customer data. Not surprisingly, the CRM investments fell well short of expectations.

Even with a sound plan for sequencing, firms have to consider the timing of their investments. They must ask themselves, in particular, one crucial question: Should we lead or follow IT trends? In making this decision, firms must understand that IT alone is almost never a true differentiator. As we saw with JP Morgan Chase's DealerTrack system, IT provides distinction only when coupled with other, less replicable advantages, such as scale or a strong brand.

A company should rush an investment, therefore, only when it's clear that the technology will advance the firm's business goals, enable true innovation that strengthens existing advantages, and be resistant to the leveling effect of imitation. In semiconductors, where superior chip design confers a major edge, Intel's investment in the development of the Pentium processor to replace the 486 proved essential to staying ahead of the competition. In semiconductor equipment, Applied Materials' aggressive investments in new manufacturing technologies also paid off, simply because its smaller rivals lacked the resources to rapidly imitate the advances.

Of course, it's hard to foresee whether an investment will yield innovative results. At the critical moment of decision, managers must be alert for red flags indicating that the investment will not differentiate the firm, such as widespread hype about the IT opportunity or a rolling wave of competitors considering it. Such signals of broad awareness suggest that any added profitability from the innovation will quickly dissipate. Companies must also know themselves: their taste for risk, their confidence that they can merge IT with other advantages to stay ahead of the pack, and their corporate track record in mobilizing people and processes to effect change. Where the indicators are weak, the best course is usually to follow, not lead.

Pursue managerial and technological innovations in tandem

History shows that technological innovations are typically of little use until managerial practices adapt to them. That was certainly true in the 1990s, and it remains true today. Wal-Mart, for instance, would have gained little from its investments in innovative information systems if it hadn't also redefined its relationships with suppliers and dramatically simplified the logistics practices at its distribution centers. Best Buy and Target would not have become leaders in retailing if they hadn't combined advanced IT with collaborative purchasing systems and advances in warehouse automation, cross-docking, and inventory tracking. Intel's IT investments turbocharged its productivity because they accompanied breakthroughs in materials technology and manufacturing processes. In all these cases, business managers led the way, reshaping their companies' processes and practices so that the full benefits of new information systems could be realized.

CRM in retail banking provides the cautionary tale. Banks hoped that the new systems for gathering and sharing customer information would boost cross-selling rates, reduce customer attrition, attract new customers, and increase profitability per customer. Yet despite massive spending on CRM, the number of products held by an average household at its primary bank has remained flat over the past three years. One reason for this, as already noted, was poor sequencing—the required customer data was not yet in place when the CRM systems came on-line. But many bank managers also failed to make necessary changes to their sales and marketing processes. The banks' business units continued to be organized around specific products and customer segments, hindering the integrated management of overall customer relationships. In addition, incentive structures for sales personnel undermined the kind of cross-selling that CRM theoretically makes possible.

The success of IT investments hinges on the particular characteristics of different industries and the particular practices of different companies. That fact goes a long way toward explaining the lack of correlation between IT spending and productivity that we've seen in recent years. For IT to fulfill its promise, users and vendors must deploy it thoughtfully, tailoring it to individual sectors and businesses and merging it with other product and process innovations. The challenge will be to use existing systems effectively while at the same time making targeted new investments that maintain competitive parity and, when possible, strengthen differentiation and buttress advantage. IT is not a silver bullet. But if it is aimed correctly, it can be an important competitive weapon.

The challenge for IT vendors

Our research revealed three practices that distinguish the companies that gained the most from their IT investments. These imperatives for effective use of IT have important implications for vendors as well.

1 **Managerial imperative: Target the productivity levers that matter.**

   Vendor response: Gain customer-specific know-how, and focus development and sales efforts on specific sectors and business models.
   IT providers must learn more about how their technology can enhance each customer's business. Whether they are helping to improve retail supply chains, cut processing time for insurance claims, or reduce errors in hospital lab work, they must master the details necessary to raise their customers' productivity.
   The shotgun approach—supplying all kinds of products to all kinds of customers—will almost surely be a losing strategy

for vendors. Those with a panoply of offerings will become mired in the complexity of managing the business, and mediocre execution for all customers will likely ensue. So providers face hard choices. They must decide where to focus and, by implication, how to "right size" themselves. The good news is that the lessons of the past decade suggest that vendors can gain valuable benefits by addressing well-defined customer segments whose performance they can really improve.

2 **Managerial imperative: Get the sequencing and timing right.**

Vendor response: Help customers find value in sunken IT investments.

Many companies with apparently lifeless IT investments may be missing one final piece of technology. So IT vendors must develop solutions to help their customers turn around unsuccessful technology deployments and articulate and deliver a clear value proposition for future investments. Unless they do both, customers will be less likely to accept big up-front costs for software and hardware in the future.

3 **Managerial imperative: Pursue managerial and technological innovations in tandem.**

Vendor response: Innovate selectively, and form learning partnerships with customers and third parties.

Technology-driven innovation will remain vital, but as companies grasp the need for simultaneous managerial innovation, their IT investments will become much more selective. In this environment, partnering to learn is vital. Vendors in retail banking, for example, can build long-term partnerships with banks by working with them to identify and execute the business changes necessary to fully benefit from investments such as data warehouses, CRM, customer data integration, and online banking. Many customers made large infrastructure investments over the past five to eight years, and they want new products and services that leverage the assets they already have.

Partnering with third parties can also help vendors tie their technical innovations with managerial breakthroughs. To achieve the highest value from IT investments, buyers need to make critical improvements in their business processes and organizational structures. An integrated information system will achieve little, for instance, if business units continue to be managed in isolation without any cross-unit incentives or reviews. By partnering with firms that specialize in redesigning processes and managing change, successful IT vendors will help ensure that their customers reap the full benefits of their new systems.

Diana Farrell,
Harvard Business Review, October 2003

2

Getting IT spending
right this time

Diana Farrell, Terra Terwilliger, and Allen P. Webb

IDEAS IN BRIEF

IT most effectively stimulates productivity by helping companies
to innovate.

To foster innovation rather than merely spawn systems that are
quickly imitated or promote the wrong goals, companies should
focus on two priorities: the first is to identify those IT investments that offer the greatest opportunities for competitive
differentiation; the second is to master the sequence and timing
of investments.

A smart approach to IT that emphasizes innovation, differentiation, and productivity requires senior executives to help set the
technology agenda and be accountable for its results.

Who can blame business technology executives if half a decade of overspending on IT now makes them somewhat obsessed by costs? Indeed, companies in much of the world are capping their IT expenditures. Some companies even peg the performance bonuses of chief information officers to how much money they cut from technology budgets.[1]

Yet companies underinvest in technology at their peril—even in lean times. New technology, deployed intelligently, can help organizations make dramatic leaps in productivity and redefine competition within whole sectors, as Wal-Mart and Dell Computer, among others, have shown. The essence of smart deployment is knowing where and when to invest. Which technology expenditures will yield a sustainable, differentiable advantage? Will the bleeding edge of technology bolster a company's bid to be a leader, or should executives wait until the risks and costs fall? These perennially difficult questions—which hinge on a complex array of industry-specific factors—become even thornier when earnings pressures are high.

Compounding the challenge is the tendency to view technology, first, as a panacea and, then, after the hype proves unrealistic, as anathema. The experience of the leaders shows that new technology alone won't boost productivity. Productivity gains come from managerial innovation: fundamental changes in the way companies deliver products or services. Companies generate innovations, in fat years or lean, by deploying new technology along with improved processes and capabilities.[2]

Priorities for investment

How can companies invest in technology to achieve meaningful gains? The McKinsey Global Institute (MGI) spent two years investigating the relationship between IT and productivity and found that the former most effectively stimulates the growth of the latter by helping companies to innovate. Innovation sometimes means creating new products (such as faster microprocessors), services (mobile telephony), or processes (on-line securities trading). But it also involves using technology to turbocharge existing processes by helping companies to extend their current advantages in key areas. When Wal-Mart linked IT with its efficient distribution network, it advanced both the state of the art in supply chain management and the productivity frontier of its sector.[3]

MGI's research suggests that to foster innovation rather than merely spawn systems that are quickly imitated or promote the wrong goals, companies should focus on two priorities. The first is to identify the productivity levers offering the greatest opportunity for competitive differentiation: targeting the few specific levers that could well create a competitive advantage produces results more reliably than striving for improvement everywhere. The most promising IT initiatives usually evolve along with related business processes and build on an organization's operational strengths. When taking this route, companies should beware the siren song of IT success stories from other industries, since the levers that matter in one sector may be irrelevant in another.

The second priority is to master the sequence and timing of investments. Many technology-based advantages, particularly those that don't involve fundamental business changes, have a limited life because they diffuse rapidly through the sector. Timing is therefore critical if IT investments are to generate returns. Companies that get it right develop a clear understanding of how IT-enabled competition is evolving in their sectors. Investing ahead of the pack makes sense if the technology is hard to mimic, continues to yield benefits even if imitated, or offers great near-term value. Otherwise, companies can often hold down their spending and boost their returns by diving in only after others have made investments—and mistakes.

Responsibility for addressing these two priorities lies with technologists and business executives alike. An IT organization needs help to have a thorough understanding of the sources of a company's productivity advantage and the competitive dynamics that influence the diffusion of technology. A smart approach to IT that emphasizes innovation, differentiation, and productivity thus requires senior executives to help set the technology agenda and be accountable for its results.

Innovation and diffusion

Our insights into the chemistry between effective IT investment and productivity build on earlier MGI research into the impressive US productivity gains achieved since 1995. Productivity, this study[4] concluded, flourishes when competition becomes so intense that managers must innovate and competitors must adopt innovations quickly. Productivity boomed in the wholesale pharmaceutical sector, for example, when downstream retail consolidation squeezed wholesalers, forcing them to achieve major efficiencies by automating their warehouses.

The rapid diffusion of technology may be good for economies, but companies derive the greatest advantage from innovations

when competitors can't adopt them quickly. Once many companies in a sector have implemented a set of IT applications, they
become just another cost of doing business, not sources of competitive advantage. Naturally, competitors can most readily
adopt the simplest IT-enabled improvements—those that primarily involve dropping a technology into place.

In retailing, for instance, central support systems, warehouse-
management and -automation systems, and point-of-sale (POS)
upgrades are now core IT investments that every large company
makes. Although they do improve productivity for the whole sector, they confer no differentiating competitive advantage on individual companies; the benefits accrue to consumers, who enjoy
lower prices and more convenient shopping. In the most extreme
cases of rapid diffusion, competitors adopt similar technologies
in a "me-too" investment frenzy; think of customer-relationship-
management (CRM) and enterprise-resource-planning (ERP) software in the late 1990s.

But some technology initiatives either *do* generate new products, processes, and services or substantially extend a company's
existing advantages. Some of these innovations don't diffuse
rapidly, because embedded in them are barriers that reduce the
competition's ability to follow suit. Such barriers arise, for instance, when IT innovations are fused with broader changes in
business processes or coupled with other, more sustainable advantages, such as economies of scale and scope or deep intellectual capital. Of course, the use of IT to generate innovations that
enhance productivity and defy imitation poses important strategic questions. How, for example, should a company seek out investments that genuinely differentiate it from competitors? How
can it plan the timing and level of investment to derive long-term
value amid fierce competition?

Investing to differentiate

To find distinctive IT investments, companies should examine operational levers with the potential to affect productivity substantially (see "The operational levers that matter"). Each lever is distinct yet sufficiently broad to encompass a range of potentially valuable opportunities. Some levers are more critical than others; moreover, their importance can vary widely by sector and even by subsector or business model. Among the levers that matter, companies should determine which ones would yield a real competitive advantage if they served as the basis for new investments; often these levers evolve with and build on existing operational strengths. In a world of scarce IT resources, it is

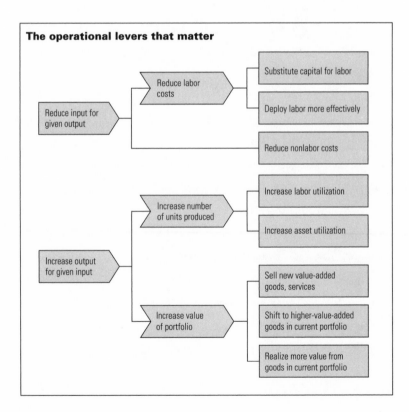

The operational levers that matter

Reduce input for given output	
	Reduce labor costs
	Substitute capital for labor
	Deploy labor more effectively
	Reduce nonlabor costs
Increase output for given input	
	Increase number of units produced
	Increase labor utilization
	Increase asset utilization
	Increase value of portfolio
	Sell new value-added goods, services
	Shift to higher-value-added goods in current portfolio
	Realize more value from goods in current portfolio

vital to know where—and where not—to target resources most intensively.

Indeed, some of the most impressive productivity gains come through a focus on a single lever. In the microprocessor subsector, for instance, major players, particularly Intel, have concentrated on new, higher-value goods, thereby generating extraordinary productivity advances as microprocessors and memory chips became exponentially more powerful though not exponentially more expensive. IT—for example, electronic-design-automation tools—played a vital role in helping manufacturers to design more complex chips and to make them more quickly, thereby powerfully underscoring the benefit of investments that target specific high-potential levers (see "Tools that save time").

The trick, of course, is to target the right levers. During the 1990s, for instance, IT had its greatest impact on the retail-banking sector by helping to automate manual processes, on the retail home-improvement subsector by making employees more efficient, and on the dynamic-random-access-memory (DRAM) segment of the semiconductor sector by boosting output.

IT systems aimed at other levers, such as the more effective deployment of labor in semiconductor fabrication facilities, had less impact even when implemented effectively.

Identifying the right levers requires an understanding, first, of the complex factors that drive the economics of individual companies and of the sector as a whole and, second, of the way IT can influence those key factors. The retail sector provides an example. Although Wal-Mart is the King Kong of general-merchandise retailers, slavishly emulating its approach to IT may be a losing strategy for retailers in other subsectors. General merchandising is characterized by low margins, large numbers of stock-keeping units, and high sales velocities—considerations that make it very

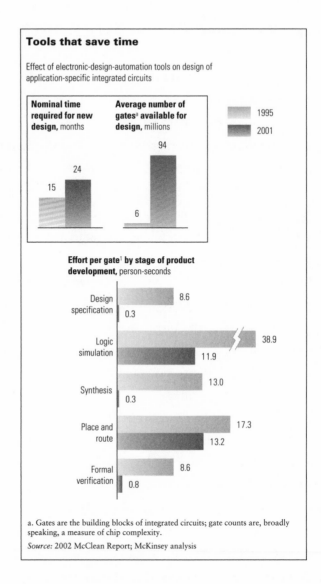

Tools that save time

Effect of electronic-design-automation tools on design of application-specific integrated circuits

Nominal time required for new design, months	Average number of gates[a] available for design, millions	
15 / 24	6 / 94	▨ 1995 ▨ 2001

Effort per gate[1] by stage of product development, person-seconds

	1995	2001
Design specification	8.6	0.3
Logic simulation	38.9	11.9
Synthesis	13.0	0.3
Place and route	17.3	13.2
Formal verification	8.6	0.8

a. Gates are the building blocks of integrated circuits; gate counts are, broadly speaking, a measure of chip complexity.

Source: 2002 McClean Report; McKinsey analysis

important to cut the time goods spend sitting in warehouses. Sophisticated warehouse- and transport-management systems are thus absolute priorities for general merchandisers.

But the retailing of apparel is different. Premium merchants such as Neiman Marcus and Saks Fifth Avenue enjoy larger margins but must cope with the unpredictability of fashion trends and a seasonally changing assortment of goods. Of course, apparel retailers need efficient distribution, but some of their most promising opportunities involve the reduction of discounts. Industry experts suggest that apparel retailers sell 50 to 80 percent of their fashion items during the first four weeks of a new season. Discounting then sets in. Apparel retailers need both forecasting systems to predict demand and applications that help fine-tune these discounting campaigns. The bottom-line impact can be significant: one expert estimates that a good demand-forecasting system can increase the number of items sold at full price by more than 25 percent.

Companies are unlikely to match their sector's leaders in all productivity levers, but shortfalls are no reason to invest heavily in every weak area. Instead, where technology and know-how are widely available, the right approach is to close performance gaps by using reliable, low-cost techniques such as implementing standard off-the-shelf applications or outsourcing business processes. When Wal-Mart, for example, acquired 122 Canadian Woolco stores, in 1994, it didn't buy Woolco's underperforming distribution assets, preferring to outsource warehouse management and transportation. Only by limiting any investment that doesn't differentiate can companies hope to become truly distinctive in the areas that matter most for them.

Conversely, intensive investment and even customization can make sense when they might produce lasting advantages. Wal-Mart originally achieved success in supply chain systems not by implementing standard software but by creating customized systems with the help of smaller vendors. This approach not only allowed the company to tailor the systems to its business needs rather than change its business processes to exploit the capabilities of the software but also made the systems and the processes they supported harder for competitors to duplicate. What is more, Wal-Mart didn't create its own IT systems across the organization; it invested selectively. The key to success was its recognition that emerging technologies created a chance to build on existing operational strengths—particularly its highly efficient distribution network—by further optimizing sourcing and delivery.

The Wal-Mart story is far from unique. High-impact investments often evolve with and extend a company's advantage. JP Morgan Chase, for example, recently used IT to augment its strengths in the automotive-finance market. The company already had more than 9,600 dealers in its system by early 2001 and was a leader in the prime-lending segment. It then began expanding its distribution network further: together with Ameri-Credit and Wells Fargo, its LabMorgan subsidiary created DealerTrack, which permits dealers to help customers find and close loans on-line. DealerTrack's automated car-finance origination and processing system is open to other banks. But since JP Morgan Chase's scale makes it possible to offer low-cost loans in the prime-lending segment, the company continues to capture benefits as DealerTrack broadens its reach, today exceeding 18,000 dealers.

Investments that pull a company's key levers—particularly investments linked to scale and other operational strengths—should influence performance measurably. Although the impact of IT on a function can be hard to isolate, rough metrics are bound to exist if the business goals are clear. (An inability to determine in advance how to measure an investment's business impact is a warning sign.) Inventory turns are an example of a rough but useful metric: when Wal-Mart bettered its performance from 6.6 in 1994 to 9.9 in 2001, the improvement showed that its RetailLink vendor-management system was on the right track. Kmart's more modest improvement (to 5.9, from 4.7) over the same period reflected the difficulty of emulating IT capabilities that extend the sector leader's existing operational advantages.

Timing and sequencing

For companies competing on the basis of IT-enabled advances, knowing when to jump onto the innovation racetrack can be as important as how. Timing and sequencing, at their simplest, ensure that all prerequisite investments are in place before new IT initiatives are launched. Particularly in the retail sector, our research highlighted the importance of multiple tiers of investment, each laying the foundation for the next. In general merchandising, for example, before companies can implement sophisticated planning applications, a certain level of competence in warehouse- and transport-management systems is needed to get goods to customers.

Thus, companies that invest in sophisticated capabilities before the fundamentals are solid can easily waste money. One major general-merchandise retailer, for instance, invested millions to manage and measure the effectiveness of sales promotions, but since its warehousing systems couldn't cope with the fluctuations in volume that accompany big promotions, it ended up with dissatisfied customers. Yet companies can also spend too much time and money on basic IT infrastructure and never reach the incremental high-return investments. Sequencing is a delicate balancing act.

Even with investments in place, companies must ask a strategic-timing question: should they lead or follow IT trends? There is a clear case for rapid action when an IT initiative is closely linked to business goals and truly innovates—either by contributing to new products, services, or processes or by improving existing processes to extend a company's advantage. Similarly compelling are investments that continue to generate benefits even if imitated.

All these conditions existed when credit-fraud-detection capabilities emerged in the retail-banking industry, in the mid-1990s. The opportunity to reduce fraud losses resulted from a series of software breakthroughs, such as advanced neural networks and predictive transaction risk models, that created sophisticated new ways of tracking customer-behavior data.[5] The magnitude of fraud losses not only justified experiments with the new software but also led managers to develop responsive new customer-contact processes to validate or reject suspicious transactions—an example of managerial and technical coevolution. The widespread adoption of the new systems didn't diminish their impact on individual companies. By 2000, fraud losses for the whole sector had fallen to 0.18 percent of gross receivables, compared with 0.41 percent in 1994, and banks shared in the gains to the extent that they contributed to them.

The experience of JP Morgan Chase with DealerTrack shows how fruitful IT leadership can be when fused with other strengths. DealerTrack's broad reach helps JP Morgan Chase serve dealers and customers more quickly. The result is a virtuous cycle of growth that extends the company's enduring strengths.

By contrast, first movers have difficulty recouping the high cost of pioneering efforts when they are neither innovative nor hard to imitate. Restraint may make sense in these situations, but how can they be recognized? Consider another retail-banking initiative: CRM. Banks hoped that these new processes for gathering and disseminating customer information would help them increase their cross-selling rates, reduce the attrition of customers, attract new ones, and increase profitability per customer. Yet the process improvements inherent in CRM haven't yielded the desired results: the number of products held by an average household at its primary bank has remained flat over the past three years despite massive spending (see "Results from easily imitated improvements fall short"). While some implementations have been difficult, an important reason for CRM's

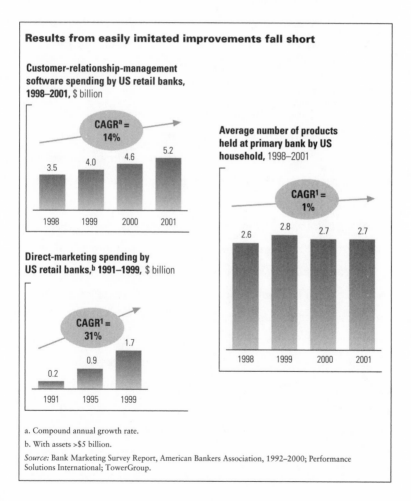

Results from easily imitated improvements fall short

Customer-relationship-management software spending by US retail banks, 1998–2001, $ billion

CAGR[a] = 14%

3.5   4.0   4.6   5.2

1998 1999 2000 2001

Average number of products held at primary bank by US household, 1998–2001

CAGR[1] = 1%

2.6   2.8   2.7   2.7

1998 1999 2000 2001

Direct-marketing spending by US retail banks,[b] 1991–1999, $ billion

CAGR[1] = 31%

0.2   0.9   1.7

1991 1995 1999

a. Compound annual growth rate.

b. With assets >$5 billion.

Source: Bank Marketing Survey Report, American Bankers Association, 1992–2000; Performance Solutions International; TowerGroup.

tendency to produce little but customer churn is that many banks simultaneously launched similar initiatives in a slow-growing market. Banks that failed to make any CRM investments might have lost customers. Yet among the institutions that did invest, the pioneers have difficulty distinguishing their results from those of banks that followed.

In fact, it can be challenging to tell beforehand whether an investment will yield innovative results. Two imperatives should guide companies making the difficult decision to pursue or yield leadership of a particular IT opportunity. The first is to look hard for signs that rapid diffusion is possible. In the case of CRM, the red flags included the sheer magnitude of the early hype, the large number of banks that consequently began implementations, and the emergence of a few software vendors with integrated product suites promising great future potential.

The second imperative is to recognize that the characteristics of a company can help it determine whether it is an appropriate leader in a given investment area. Having identified an opportunity for innovation, a company must ask itself how much appetite for risk it has in that part of the business, how confident it is that it can link the investment to other advantages and thereby stay ahead of the pack, and what sort of track record it has in putting people and processes in place to effect change. Where the answers are discouraging, the best option is usually to follow, not lead. Companies that foreswear low-cost follower strategies are squandering scarce resources that might be used more effectively to pull operational levers that could create a clear productivity advantage. After all, the goal is not to be the first to seize all IT-enabled productivity opportunities but rather to place smart bets on the right ones. Companies can improve their odds of success by evaluating themselves as well as their investments.

Smart IT investing doesn't require a return to the spendthrift ways of the late 1990s. Companies that understand where to focus and how to time their efforts can find IT investments that will not only differentiate them from competitors but also provide a lasting competitive advantage—and avoid investments that won't.

This article is based on a collaborative study undertaken by the McKinsey Global Institute, McKinsey's high-technology practice, and McKinsey's Business Technology Office. Shyam Lal, James Manyika, Lenny Mendonca, Mike Nevens, and Roger Roberts helped lead the project. The research team, which deserves special recognition, included Anil Kale, Mukund Ramaratnam, Eva Rzepniewski, and Nick Santhanam.

Diana Farrell, Terra Terwilliger, and Allen P. Webb,
McKinsey Quarterly, 2003 Number 2

Notes

1. "Thrift shop," *Information Week,* December 23, 2002, pp. 18–19.

2. See William W. Lewis, Vincent Palmade, Baudouin Regout, and Allen P. Webb, "What's right with the US economy," *The McKinsey Quarterly,* 2002 Number 1, pp. 30–40 (www.mckinseyquarterly.com/links/3896); and Diana Farrell, Heino Fassbender, Thomas Kneip, Stephan Kriesel, and Eric Labaye, "Reviving French and German productivity," *The McKinsey Quarterly,* 2003 Number 1, pp. 40–55 (www.mckinseyquarterly.com/links/4724).

3. MGI's newest report—the basis of this article—is *How IT Enables Productivity Growth,* McKinsey Global Institute, Washington, DC, November 2002. It focuses on IT's role in facilitating productivity gains in three high-performing US sectors during the 1990s: retailing, semiconductors, and retail banking.

4. *US Productivity Growth 1995–2000* (McKinsey Global Institute, Washington, DC, October 2001), which also emphasizes that regulatory changes can spur the competition that drives innovation.

5. See Corey Booth and Shashi Buluswar, "The return of artificial intelligence," *The McKinsey Quarterly,* 2002 Number 4, pp. 98–105 (www.mckinseyquarterly.com/links/4726).

3

A road map for European economic reform

Martin Neil Baily and Diana Farrell

IDEAS IN BRIEF

Europe's politicians are in a fix. The main reason is the poor economic performance of several of the European Union's larger countries.

Many Europeans believe that regulatory reforms to make their product and labor markets more competitive will entail eliminating their social safety nets. As alternatives to reform, some advocate protectionist policies, others more investment in R&D.

However, such reforms will spur the productivity growth Europe needs in order to recover the prosperity that underpins its social safety nets. Keeping the nets in place depends on undertaking regulatory reforms to boost competition.

The European Union's recent economic performance has been dismal. Growth in the region's core economies remains sluggish, and the budgets of some countries are in deficit—a problem that threatens to get worse as their populations age.[1] One member of the European commission summed up the problems thus: "We cannot accept 17 million unemployed, average economic growth of 0.6 percent in the old member states, and youth unemployed of 18.6 percent in the 25-member European Union."[2] Europe's leaders agree that they must boost the region's economy and meet the challenges of global competition. The trouble is, no one can agree how.

Many European officials believe that competition and market forces are actually hindering economic growth and that reform will mean the elimination of Europe's social safety net. Their solution is to protect the region against competition, to maintain regulations that prevent companies from restructuring and making layoffs, and, perhaps, to invest more money in research and development.

History proves, however, that such solutions won't work. No dynamic, growing, full-employment economy in the world also maintains rigid regulations and restrictions on competition. The McKinsey Global Institute (MGI) studied six major European countries and found that their low rate of economic growth was not caused by a lack of technology. Instead, boosting competition, often through regulatory reform, is the impetus that Europe needs to improve its productivity.

Europe won't have to abandon its social programs, however. Many European countries may have to modify their social-benefits programs in order to restore the incentive to work, but, as Denmark has shown, governments can provide income support to the unemployed while encouraging them to find new jobs. Paradoxically, Europe must restore full employment and generate economic growth if it is to have the funding for adequate pensions and social insurance, especially as the population ages.

Ideally, Europe's low-performing nations would embrace economic reform. Not all of them are willing to go down that road yet, unfortunately. While no country has fully liberalized its economy, Denmark, Ireland, Spain, Sweden, and the United Kingdom have undertaken reforms that have stimulated more employment and growth. These countries set an example by combining better economic performance with preserving the essentials of the European way of life.

Competition is the key to growth

MGI's research on a range of European economies shows that deregulation or regulatory reform improves productivity. In every one of the countries we studied, a gap exists between the productivity of the majority of companies in a given industry and those that followed best practice. France and Germany provide a good example.[3] For most industries, labor productivity is lower in France and Germany than in the United States (see "The productivity gap"). Food retailing in France and mobile telecoms in both France and Germany are the only exceptions (see "The exception proves the rule"). While a number of

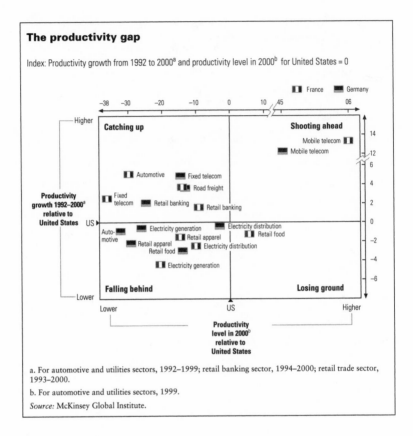

The productivity gap

Index: Productivity growth from 1992 to 2000[a] and productivity level in 2000[b] for United States = 0

a. For automotive and utilities sectors, 1992–1999; retail banking sector, 1994–2000; retail trade sector, 1993–2000.

b. For automotive and utilities sectors, 1999.

Source: McKinsey Global Institute.

European industries closed the productivity gap with the United States during the 1990s, about as many fell further behind—a worrisome trend.

Regulations stifle competition

What prevents Europe's productivity from reaching its potential? The gap in some industries is caused by structural differences. In retailing, for example, small proprietor-owned stores are much more common in Europe than in the United States; they are also less productive than either large discount retailers

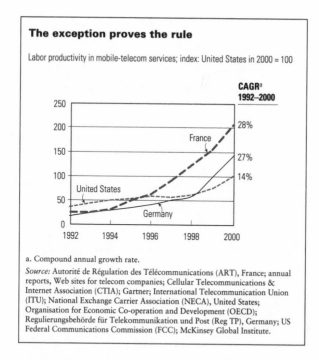

The exception proves the rule

Labor productivity in mobile-telecom services; index: United States in 2000 = 100

a. Compound annual growth rate.

Source: Autorité de Régulation des Télécommunications (ART), France; annual reports, Web sites for telecom companies; Cellular Telecommunications & Internet Association (CTIA); Gartner; International Telecommunication Union (ITU); National Exchange Carrier Association (NECA), United States; Organisation for Economic Co-operation and Development (OECD); Regulierungsbehörde für Telekommunikation und Post (Reg TP), Germany; US Federal Communications Commission (FCC); McKinsey Global Institute.

or chains of small specialty stores. In other industries, differences in productivity stem from the way production processes came about. On the one hand, French automakers adopted lean manufacturing in the 1990s, sparking rapid productivity growth. German auto companies, on the other hand, started the decade in a dominant position and felt little pressure to change. As a result, their productivity stagnated. The MGI studies found clear evidence that the differences in both structure and processes were symptoms of a deeper problem: a lack of competitive pressure.

Competition raises productivity because the companies that do best are the ones that respond by making the smartest innovations. The winners expand their market share and create more jobs, so the less productive companies must either improve or go out of business. But this dynamic is absent in Europe. In several European economies, the most productive businesses are not growing or increasing their workforce, while the less productive ones are still hiring (see "Survival of the unfittest").

The reason is that regulations on product markets and policies governing labor and the use of land have the effect of protecting incumbents, limiting new entrants, preventing companies from achieving economies of scale, and restricting the way businesses operate.

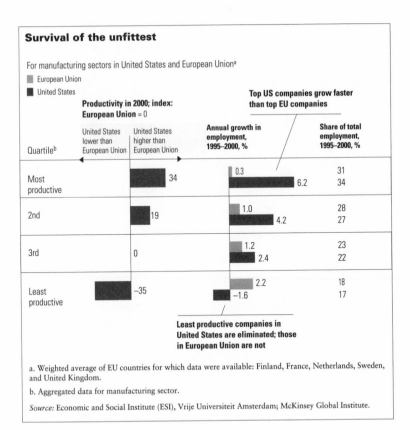

Survival of the unfittest

For manufacturing sectors in United States and European Union[a]

■ European Union
■ United States

a. Weighted average of EU countries for which data were available: Finland, France, Netherlands, Sweden, and United Kingdom.

b. Aggregated data for manufacturing sector.

Source: Economic and Social Institute (ESI), Vrije Universiteit Amsterdam; McKinsey Global Institute.

Promoting R&D and IT is not the answer

Much of the discussion in Europe focuses on policies to spur investment in IT and R&D rather than on increasing competition through regulatory reform.[4] Our research into European industries shows that the R&D approach doesn't address the source of the problem.[5]

European leaders stress the need for R&D because they see how the US high-tech sector, which boasted double-digit productivity increases each year over the course of the 1990s, has benefited the US economy. But the impact of this sector on the overall economy is often overstated: it accounted for only about a third of the growth differential between Europe and the United States during the late 1990s. Most of the gap in productivity growth was the result of industries other than IT.

When MGI compared European and US industries that use IT, we found that access to IT and the employees' level of proficiency with it were not major reasons for the differences in performance. For one thing, many industries in Europe have already widely adopted the productivity-enhancing technologies used by their global competitors. Those that haven't are limited by regulations that prevent them from making large-scale investments in IT or by labor laws that restrict the layoffs that could result from the use of technology. Regulatory reform is the best way to increase its use: under competitive pressure, companies will adopt the technologies that can help them to survive and prosper.

The MGI studies strongly support the case for reforming regulations that constrain how European companies operate and compete and that interrupt the virtuous cycle of competition, innovation, and productivity growth. Investments in R&D and IT should be based on realistic estimates of returns, not as an excuse to avoid the politically difficult task of economic reform.

The path to reform in Europe

The goal of economic regulation should be to ensure fair competition. At the same time, regulation must protect consumers, the environment, and a society's more vulnerable citizens from market failures. Parts of Europe's current regulatory framework focus on protecting society to the detriment of competition, perversely making Europeans more susceptible to the consequences of the region's flagging competitiveness.[6]

The good news is that policymakers can often achieve their social objectives without restricting productivity and growth. Four areas of reform are critical. While these suggestions aren't new, they are worth repeating, given the disagreement in policy circles about what hinders Europe's competitiveness.

Finish liberalizing the service sector

Service industries—everything from hairdressers and retail stores to accountants and engineers—accounted for roughly 70 percent of Europe's GDP and all of its net job growth during the past five years. Manufacturing is not going to be a major source of new jobs in Europe or any mature economy, regardless of how much money governments pump into R&D. For Europe, revitalizing its service industries will be the key to boosting economic growth and employment levels.

In service industries, however, national and often local companies remain shielded by a thicket of regulatory barriers. In

Germany, for example, limits on operating hours prevent retailers from providing the more convenient service and higher employment that would result from remaining open longer. In Portugal, the government requires hotels to employ a set number of staff in each job category, depending on the hotel's size. Across the Continent, small family-run corner shops with low productivity and relatively high prices are protected by tax and zoning laws.

Regulations such as these aim to preserve the unique culture, traditions, and lifestyle of Europe, but they have the effect of limiting prosperity—on which the region's cultural continuity ultimately depends. Fortunately, adjusting the level of regulation to increase competition in service sectors doesn't mean abandoning all the old traditions. If Germany were to lift restrictions on the hours that stores can remain open, not all consumers would shop around the clock and small stores offering a unique service would still prosper. If individual hotels in Portugal didn't have to maintain such a large workforce, employment across the industry would increase, since more entrepreneurs would build and operate hotels. Removing the regulations that protect small but inefficient retail stores will not drive these businesses out of Europe, because a sufficient number of consumers patronize them.

The EU Services Directive, proposed last year, would remove national regulatory barriers and liberalize cross-border competition and trade in services. By creating a common market for services, companies could consolidate and gain scale, thus reducing prices and increasing productivity. A report by *Copenhagen Economics* found that liberalizing the service industries would create up to 600,000 jobs in Europe and stimulate €33 billion worth of new economic activity each year.[7] The directive came under fierce attack, and revisions are inevitable. Yet the essential goal should remain: to create a single competitive market for services in Europe.

Encourage economies of scale

Enabling companies to achieve economies of scale is one of the most important ways countries can boost their productivity growth; indeed, this goal was one major reason Europe created a common market in the first place. Policymakers can encourage the efficient use of scale in two ways: by facilitating mergers and acquisitions and by standardizing regulations across the European Union so that companies can expand easily into other national markets.

Antitrust regulations rightly seek to prevent mergers that would create monopolies. But regulations that restrict mergers unnecessarily—such as those governing Germany's many small regional banks—have the effect of allowing inefficient operators to stay in business when newcomers could provide the same services more efficiently (see "Small can equal inefficient").

In principle, the rules adopted by the European Union in 2004 already allow companies greater freedom in M&A. But a proposed ban on multiple voting rights and unapproved poison pills was made optional, in deference to those member states that thought hostile acquisitions would undermine their brand of capitalism (which gives stakeholders other than shareholders a say in corporate governance).[8] And inefficient incumbents— the potential takeover targets—lobbied their governments hardest of all to block the ban. Such companies remain protected at the cost of true competition.

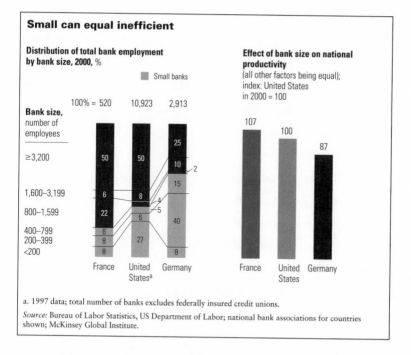

Small can equal inefficient

Distribution of total bank employment by bank size, 2000, %

Effect of bank size on national productivity (all other factors being equal); index: United States in 2000 = 100

a. 1997 data; total number of banks excludes federally insured credit unions.

Source: Bureau of Labor Statistics, US Department of Labor; national bank associations for countries shown; McKinsey Global Institute.

Establishing uniform EU regulations can also allow the kind of cross-border expansion that unleashes rapid productivity growth. Europe's road freight industry is a good example. Its deregulation in the 1990s sparked a wave of consolidation, and long-haul routes are now more efficient across the Continent. Larger-scale companies are better able to deploy expensive tools, such as route optimization systems, and capacity utilization and productivity have increased dramatically.

Increase work incentives and labor market flexibility

Unemployment across the European Union remains stubbornly high, particularly among the young and those near retirement age. This may seem odd, since so many countries have strict labor laws in place to protect jobs. Yet restrictions on laying people off, plus high taxes on employment to finance generous social-security benefits, deter companies from hiring new people. And these benefits, depending on how they are structured, can lower the incentive to work. An overhaul of Europe's labor regulations should aim to promote job creation and employment as well as to smooth the transition of workers between jobs.

France's minimum wage, for example, is twice that of the United States, and strict regulations on hiring and firing workers have a chilling effect on employment levels. French retailers, for instance, employ 50 percent fewer workers, as a percentage of the population, than do their US counterparts. The European view that anyone holding a full-time job should be able to support a family appeals to a sense of fairness. If all employers are required to pay high-skill wages for low-skill work, however, more jobs will disappear. Procedures are a problem too: hotels in France have to maintain a small army of lawyers to deal with complex labor regulations. Not surprisingly, these laws curtail employment and do little to improve customer service. Giving companies the freedom to hire and fire employees and to negotiate salaries will actually boost job creation overall in Europe's economy.

Europe also needs to adjust its generous unemployment benefits so that they don't deter people from working. In the Netherlands, for example, a 60-year-old person receiving jobless benefits stands to lose 90 percent of any extra income that taking a job would provide.[9] Countries can encourage people to move into, or return to, the workforce without removing the social safety net. Permitting employers to pay lower salaries for some jobs but asking the government to make up the difference with a wage subsidy would encourage people to move off welfare into work, irrespective of the pay.

End the bias in land-use policies

Within the relatively small confines of Europe's borders lie important historical sites and immense natural beauty, and Europeans understandably want to preserve this heritage. Few people realize, however, the extent to which restrictions on the use of land are discouraging productivity and employment.

The high price and lack of available land, as well as other regulatory barriers, constrain companies from expanding and creating new opportunities. Carrefour and IKEA have had difficulty finding new locations for their large stores, for example, thus holding back productivity and employment in the retail sector throughout Europe—notably in Germany, where a license is required even to convert an existing building to retail use. The bureaucracy alone can be a problem. In France, it takes ten administrative procedures and nearly 200 days just to register a sizable business property, even when no zoning changes are required. By contrast, in Sweden this type of registration takes only 2 days. Even though most European policymakers say they want to increase the number of manufacturing jobs, it can take months or even years for companies to get approval to build a new factory. Moreover, the costs of construction are often inflated by a variety of regulations. The same applies to new housing development, and the resulting shortage of new construction raises housing costs and makes workers wary of relocating to find work.

Zoning decisions should aim to encourage economic growth while protecting the environment and to balance the two priorities appropriately when conflicts arise. At present, European land-use policies are biased against development. One reason is that the local officials in charge of granting building permits have no incentive to encourage investment or job creation, since state and central governments receive most of the taxes from new businesses. Sometimes local authorities deny building permits in response to pressure from incumbent companies that want to block new competitors from moving in.

The residential-housing market in the Netherlands provides one example where Europe's approach to zoning has promoted productivity. The key for developers is acquiring large plots of land, thus allowing for economies of scale. By frequently using land reclaimed from the North Sea, the Netherlands has been able to boost its productivity in home building—a huge job creator and an engine of output for all economies—to a level comparable to that of the United States.

Looking ahead

Europe can get its economy moving again without abandoning all the social values it holds dear. Many of Europe's current regulations, while aimed at preserving those values, are hindering the region's ability to compete in global markets. They need a thorough overhaul.

At times the European Commission has been a source of pressure for reform and for greater competition. And it still can push for the liberalization of markets, through its policies on competition and perhaps the introduction of a new services directive to replace the recently rejected one. But national governments must take the initiative.

Some countries have already made great strides. Ireland and Spain have experienced strong growth. The United Kingdom enjoys full employment and, by such measures as per capita income, has overtaken France and Germany. In the 1980s Denmark and Sweden undertook labor market reforms that helped them to reduce unemployment. And the new Eastern European entrants to the European Union are transforming themselves by liberalizing their markets.

Even if Europe doesn't progress in unison, one country's successful reforms can point the way to better economic performance for all of the others while preserving the essentials of the European way of life. If enough governments start to move in the right direction, the rest of Europe will surely follow.

Martin Neil Baily and Diana Farrell,
McKinsey Quarterly, Web exclusive, September 2005

Notes

1. Diana Farrell, "The economic impact of an aging Europe." *The McKinsey Quarterly,* Web exclusive, May 2005 (www.mckinseyquarterly .com/links/18705).

2. Vladimir Spidla, EC commissioner for employment, social affairs, and equal opportunities, the 2005 Jean-Jacques Rousseau lecture at Lisbon Council, Brussels, June 20, 2005.

3. Diana Farrell, Heino Fassbender, Thomas Kneip, Stephan Kriesel, and Eric Labaye. "Reviving French and German productivity," *The McKinsey Quarterly.* 2003 Number 1, pp. 40–55 (www.mckinseyquarterly .com/links/18697); and Martin Neil Baily and Jacob Funk Kirkegaard, *Transforming the European Economy,* Washington, DC: Institute for International Economics, 2004.

4. To that end, the European Commission recently proposed the creation of a publicly funded research institute to mimic the Massachusetts Institute of Technology, and the European Commission on Competitiveness is seeking increases in government funding for R&D.

5. Diana Farrell, "The *real* new economy," *Harvard Business Review.* October 2003, Volume 81, Number 10, pp. 105–112.

6. Scott C. Beardsley and Diana Farrell, "Regulation that's good for competition," *The McKinsey Quarterly,* 2005 Number 2, pp. 48–59 (www.mckinseyquarterly.com/links/18706).

7. "Economic assessment of the barriers to the internal market for services," *Copenhagen Economics,* January 2005.

8. "The EU takeover directive and the competitiveness of European Industry," André Nilsen, Oxford Council on Good Governance, analysis number 1.

9. *Economic Policy Reforms: Going for Growth,* Organisation for Economic Co-operation and Development, Paris, 2005.

4

Domestic services: the hidden key to growth

Diana Farrell, Martin Baily, and Jaana Remes

IDEAS IN BRIEF

Higher productivity in services is the key to growth in any economy. Local services account for more than 60 percent of all jobs in middle income and developed economies, and virtually all of new job creation.

Service jobs are not necessarily low-skill, low-wage, or ephemeral. Services comprise many activities critical to economic growth, like power supply, transport, and tele-communications, as well as numerous high-skill, high-wage occupations, such as accountants, researchers, and health and financial services professionals.

Given the right competitive environment, local services across the range can be a powerful source of wealth creation and jobs for middle-income economies—more powerful than offshore services could ever be.

Having focused for many years on manufacturing-led growth, policymakers across the developing world now recognize the contribution that service exports can make: India leads the world in offshore IT services; Dubai has tourism as well as a growing financial services hub; Singapore is building hospitals to serve patients from across Asia; the Philippines is developing call centers. Yet these offshore service strategies overlook a far larger, if less well-understood, opportunity to boost wealth creation: stimulating domestic service sectors.

Higher productivity in services is the key to growth in any economy. Local services account for more than 60 percent of all jobs in middle income and developed economies, and virtually all of new job creation (see "Service sector growth during economic evolution"). Manufacturing is not going to be a sustainable long-term source of new jobs anywhere—even in China—given the rapid advances in technology and productivity that are reducing industry's labor needs.

Why, then, do so many policymakers omit local services from their development plans? Part of the reason is that service work has a poor reputation. Low-skill, low-wage, ephemeral jobs in fast food joints and beauty parlors hardly seem the building blocks of a modern economy. But such jobs form the minority of service employment: even in the United States, widely thought to have too many of them, they represent only 22 percent of the huge range of total service employment. In fact, services comprise many activities critical to economic growth, like power supply, transport, and telecommunications, as well as numerous high-skill, high-wage occupations, such as accountants, re-

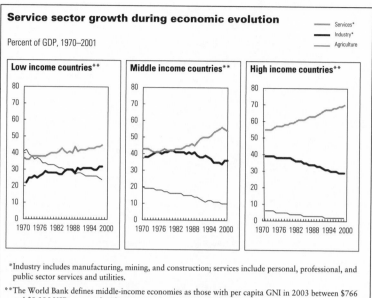

Service sector growth during economic evolution

Percent of GDP, 1970–2001

Services*
Industry*
Agriculture

Low income countries** | Middle income countries** | High income countries**

*Industry includes manufacturing, mining, and construction; services include personal, professional, and public sector services and utilities.

**The World Bank defines middle-income economies as those with per capita GNI in 2003 between $766 and $9,385 USD measured with average exchange rate over past 2 years.

Source: World Bank; World development indicators.

searchers, and professionals in health and financial services (see "What are services?").

What are services?

Market service activities in today's economies are tremendously diverse. The EU Services Directive divides them into three categories: services provided to consumers, services provided to other businesses, and services provided to both consumers and businesses.

In the United States, which is typical of a developed service economy, some 29 percent of the roughly 100 million service jobs are in consumer services, which include retail, food and accommodation services, and personal services like car repair shops, dry cleaners, and beauticians. About 77 percent of US consumer service jobs are in relatively low-skilled sales and service occupations. These jobs tend also to have a higher share of very small businesses, higher business turn-over rates, and a disproportional share of female employees.[a]

As economies grow richer, business to business services represent an increasing share of total economic activity. Today, they represent 27 percent of all US service sector employment, almost as much as consumer services. These activities include: professional services, such as law, accountancy, and consulting; technical services, such as IT and software support; wholesale trade services; and employment services like headhunters and temp agencies. The recent rapid growth in business services in developed economies is an outcome of specialization. As companies focus increasingly on their core competencies, they buy more noncore services from third parties.

Services provided to both consumers and businesses include real estate and banking, as well as services based on extensive physical networks, like telecommunications and electricity supply. These types of services account for another 7 percent of service sector jobs. The remaining 36 percent of service jobs are in nonmarket activities like healthcare, education, and public sector services.[b]

a. Foster, Haltiwanger, and Krizan (2002) "The Link Between Aggregate and Micro Productivity Growth: Evidence from Retail Trade." NBER Working Paper #9120.

b. We do not cover nonmarket services in this article. For a perspective on performance improvement potential in the public sector, see Dohrman and Mendonca, "Boosting Government Productivity" The McKinsey Quarterly, 2004 Number 4.

After years of neglect and undue regulatory constraints, local service productivity in most emerging economies lags far behind productivity in sectors developed for export. This is a pity. Research by the McKinsey Global Institute (MGI) suggests that, given the right competitive environment, local services across the range can be a powerful source of wealth creation and jobs for middle-income economies, more powerful than offshore services could ever be.

Faster growth and more good jobs

Once an economy reaches the middle income level of development, service industries become a more important source of job growth than manufacturing. And, contrary to popular belief, a substantial percentage of these jobs are high-skill and high-wage. The more dynamic and competitive an economy's service sector, the more jobs and GDP growth it will create.

More good jobs

Since 1997, employment has declined in the goods producing sectors of most developed and many developing economies, leaving service industries responsible for all net job creation (see "Services and net job growth sector contribution to overall net job growth 1997–2003"). Among middle- and high-income economies today, services generate 62 percent of all employment on average, and the higher a country's GDP per capita, the higher the share of service employment (see "Share of services is high and increases with GDP per capita").[1]

Manufacturing employment is shrinking as a result of more efficient use of labor, automation, and new IT. Roughly 22 million manufacturing jobs disappeared worldwide between 1995 and 2002, despite policy efforts to preserve them. Even China, the world's "factory floor," lost 15 million manufacturing jobs, equivalent to 15 percent of total Chinese manufacturing and a higher proportion than the global average loss of 11 percent.[2]

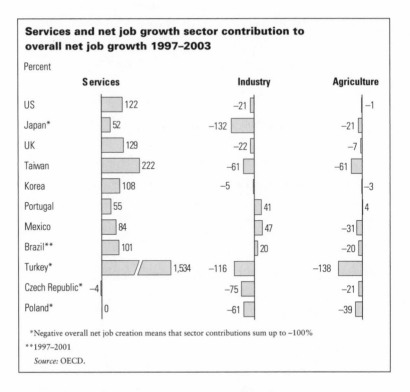

Services and net job growth sector contribution to overall net job growth 1997–2003

Percent

	Services	Industry	Agriculture
US	122	−21	−1
Japan*	52	−132	−21
UK	129	−22	−7
Taiwan	222	−61	−61
Korea	108	−5	−3
Portugal	55	41	4
Mexico	84	47	−31
Brazil**	101	20	−20
Turkey*	1,534	−116	−138
Czech Republic*	−4	−75	−21
Poland*	0	−61	−39

*Negative overall net job creation means that sector contributions sum up to −100%

**1997–2001

Source: OECD.

New jobs created by the boom in foreign manufacturing investment were not enough to offset these losses, caused largely by restructuring in China's state-owned manufacturing plants.

Somewhat surprisingly, service industries actually create more high-skilled occupations than manufacturing. In the United States, more than 30 percent of service jobs are in the highest skill category of professional, technical, managerial, and administrative occupations. In contrast, only 12 percent of all manufacturing jobs are in this category, and the same pattern holds in other developed nations.[3] There are also many well-paid "blue-collar" jobs in services, such as electricians, plumbers, and auto mechanics. In fact, the distribution of wages in the United States looks broadly similar in services and manufacturing (see "Distribution of manufacturing and service earnings is very similar").

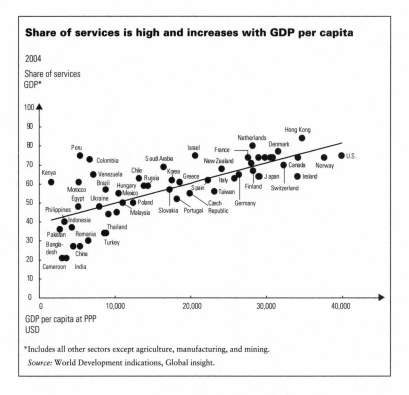

Share of services is high and increases with GDP per capita

2004
Share of services
GDP*

*Includes all other sectors except agriculture, manufacturing, and mining.
Source: World Development indications, Global insight.

There are more low-wage jobs in services, but also many high-wage jobs, and the variance within each sector is actually greater than the variance between them. Moreover, the experience of some countries in Europe shows that trying to contain growth in low-skill service jobs by imposing high minimum wages and other labor market restrictions results in higher overall unemployment, not more high-skill jobs.

Low-skill consumer service jobs, just like low-skill manufacturing jobs, may not be the most attractive. But they are crucial to all economies in providing formal employment for new entrants to the workforce and also unskilled workers—a group whose only alternatives are informal (and therefore illegal) work or welfare. Even if consumer service workers learn few value-adding skills "on the job," having a formal position can help

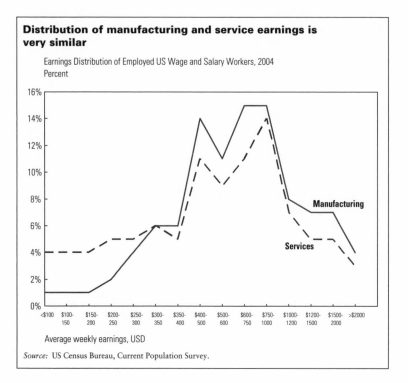

Distribution of manufacturing and service earnings is very similar

Earnings Distribution of Employed US Wage and Salary Workers, 2004
Percent

Average weekly earnings, USD

Source: US Census Bureau, Current Population Survey.

them or their dependents to study elsewhere, and so move up the occupational ladder.

Faster growth

Because of their sheer size, local service sectors like retail and construction are important drivers of overall GDP growth. And access to high quality local services affects rates of growth in all other sectors because every enterprise uses them. Good local services can also make a difference in attracting foreign direct investment (FDI). Electricity, communications, and transport quality and cost all influence the overall attractiveness of an off-shore location to multinational companies choosing where to invest. In the early 1990s, for instance, India's nascent offshore sector was hobbled by unreliable phone and Internet connections. It was only after local telecom services improved that offshoring in India took off. Indeed, MGI interviews with executives at multinationals show that they value a stronger infrastructure and reliable network services more than direct incentives from governments. Managers at Brazilian auto OEMs and Indian offshore service companies that received direct government incentives told us they would rather the money had gone on improving ports and roads in Brazil and telecommunications in India.[4]

The myths about services

Given the employment and growth benefits of a dynamic service sector, why have so few economies adopted service sector reforms? Three myths explain this anomaly.

Myth 1: There is little scope for innovation in local services, so reforming them won't do much for overall growth

History shows otherwise. Productivity improvements in service industries like electricity supply and telecommunications were important drivers of overall productivity growth in the developed economies after World War II. In the United States, the late 1990s boom in productivity was in large part due to services industries like retail, wholesale, and financial services.

Indeed, MGI's studies of countries around the world show that gaps between productivity levels in their large, employment-intensive local service sectors, such as retail and construction, explain a substantial amount of the gaps between their respective GDP per head figures. In Turkey, we found that labor productivity in manufacturing averaged 64 percent of the US level, while it was only 33 percent in services.

Retail sector reforms are particularly important in triggering productivity growth, partly because these sectors employ so many people, partly because improvements here stimulate productivity advances among upstream suppliers. For example, the liberalized retail sector in the United States has been one of the top three contributors to aggregate productivity increases since 1995.

Research has shown that removing restrictions on outlet size, opening hours, or product selection from retailers in other OECD countries would allow their retailers likewise to streamline distribution systems, and grow both sales volumes and employment. Their consumers, too, would benefit from lower prices and a broader array of services.[5]

Research elsewhere has demonstrated that liberalizing trade policies governing services generally has far higher welfare benefits for developing economies than equivalent reforms to manufacturing or agricultural policies. Even though trade barriers in services are usually lower, the economic benefits from removing them are larger because of the huge improvements in service productivity they unleash.[6]

Myth 2: Increasing service sector productivity will rapidly increase unemployment

This anxiety centers on the retail sector, a huge employer in all economies. Policymakers rightly believe that more productive supermarket and large discount formats will drive out traditional, less productive, small stores. But this is the normal process of economic development that will result in a bigger national income and higher overall employment.

MGI emerging country case studies show that in most cases net employment in retailing *increases* when the sector adopts more productive formats. Supermarkets and large-scale retailers, because of their higher productivity, can cut prices, attract more customers, and so increase their incomes. As they grow, they employ more people. Their growth also stimulates new jobs in retail supply industries, such as food processing and consumer manufacturing. In Mexico, for example, rapidly expanding formal convenience stores were the main source of employment growth in the retail sector after it was opened to foreign investment.[7] Likewise, we found that in Thailand and Poland, the net impact on employment of opening the retail sector to investment by modern format retailers was likely to be neutral or positive.[8]

This phenomenon helps explain why the share of retail in total employment is still higher in the United States, with its very small percentage of traditional retailers, than in most low- and middle-income economies, with a large proportion of retail workers employed in traditional formats (see "Share of employment in retail").

Myth 3: Services are an unreliable source of jobs

Many policymakers still believe that manufacturing jobs are not only higher skill and higher wage than service jobs but also more reliable, because the fixed costs of capital intensive plants means they are unlikely to move elsewhere. Are they?

There certainly is higher turnover in service jobs than in manufacturing jobs. But service jobs provide a much more reliable source of overall employment than manufacturing. In any given year, on average roughly 10 percent of all jobs in an economy come to an end, because workers quit or become redundant. More jobs end in services than manufacturing, particularly in

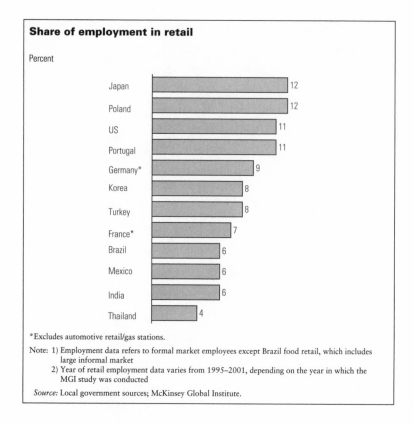

Share of employment in retail

Percent

Japan	12
Poland	12
US	11
Portugal	11
Germany*	9
Korea	8
Turkey	8
France*	7
Brazil	6
Mexico	6
India	6
Thailand	4

*Excludes automotive retail/gas stations.

Note: 1) Employment data refers to formal market employees except Brazil food retail, which includes large informal market
2) Year of retail employment data varies from 1995–2001, depending on the year in which the MGI study was conducted

Source: Local government sources; McKinsey Global Institute.

service segments dominated by small-scale operations, with their relatively high failure rates.

However, service industries as a whole create more jobs than they lose, often through the activity of new entrants.[9] Creating a dynamic service sector therefore reliably guarantees lifetime employment opportunities for everyone, if not the same job for life.

For example, from 1977–1987, the US auto repair industry lost 49 percent of its jobs, but at the same time took on new employees in jobs equivalent to 56 percent of total employment in the industry. So although almost half of all auto repair jobs ended over the period, net employment in the sector grew by 7 percent.[10] Data from middle-income economies, albeit limited, suggest their dynamics of service job destruction and creation are similar.[11]

These myths about services have led many policymakers to penalize or neglect their local service sector, usually in favor of industrial expansion. But MGI's country research has shown such choices bear considerable costs. Take Japan. By the end of the last century, Japan's world-class manufacturers of autos, steel, machine tools and consumer electronics were legendary for their performance. But their output comprised only 10 per cent of GDP. Productivity in the rest of the economy—about 68 percent of it in local services—was a dismal 63 percent of US levels.[12] Low productivity in local services goes a long way towards explaining why Japanese GDP growth tailed off in the 1990s, just as subsequent incremental reforms of service sectors help to explain the recent improvement in Japan's economic performance. Japan's Cabinet Office calculates that deregulation in telecoms, transport, energy, finance, and retailing were responsible for 4.6 percent of the country's GDP in 2002.[13]

Neglecting and overregulating service industries also has the perverse consequence of encouraging growth in the informal service sector. In many developing and middle-income economies, the majority of output in services such as retail and construction comes from informal firms that neither pay full taxes, nor abide by worker safety and other regulations, nor even register. Their unearned cost advantage allows low-productivity players to survive and prevents more productive formal companies from taking market share. In Brazil's food retail sector, for example, MGI found that tax-paying, productive, modern format retailers are at a large cost disadvantage to small, unproductive, informal players that evade tax. Acquiring the informal players is no remedy as the scale gains would be too small to offset the extra tax burden. As a result, growth in more productive, higher wage jobs in services is capped, and average productivity in Brazil's retail sector is only 16 percent of the US level.[14]

How to develop a dynamic local service sector

Government policymakers keen to unlock local services' power to generate growth and jobs must remove barriers to competition. This requires leveling the playing field so that services can compete freely for capital, labor, and technology; removing inappropriate restrictions on service businesses; and tackling informality.

Level the playing field

Governments first need to remove any remaining biases against services and give them equal treatment in fiscal, financial, and development policies. Then service companies can compete for capital and workers on the same terms as manufacturing firms.

- *Open up capital markets to local services.* Investments in services should be assessed against the same criteria as manufacturing investments. In many countries, this is not the case. Directed lending policies in banking remain prevalent. In South Korea, for instance, during its push for manufacturing-led growth, banks were prohibited outright from lending to consumer service sectors like leisure and real estate. In China today, state-owned manufacturing enterprises account for 65 percent of all loans, even though they produce just 35 percent of industrial output. Meanwhile, IPO rules in most developing countries' stock markets allow only large companies to list, thereby discriminating against service sectors that have smaller players. Policymakers need to liberalize financial systems, so they will allocate capital to the projects with highest returns, regardless of sector.

- *End industrial subsidies.* Governments often explicitly subsidize investments in manufacturing activities they consider in the national interest. For instance, Malaysia has supported the creation of the Proton in order to have a national car company. The Brazilian government offered subsidies worth $100,000 per job created to foreign carmakers to invest in local factories, prompting so much investment, the result was overcapacity and generally low productivity throughout the industry. Such subsidies not only often waste taxpayers' money, but put service industries at a disadvantage.

- *Expand favorable business conditions to cover services.* Many middle income economies have created special economic zones (SEZs) for foreign and/or export manufacturers, with more favorable tax and tariff rates and lighter regulation than domestic companies face. It makes sense to provide conditions that allow businesses to flourish, but why not extend them to all businesses? Governments should equalize regulations between sectors and set corporate taxes at affordable levels across the economy.

- *Physically integrate manufacturing and service activities.* Today's SEZs are often geographically as well as fiscally

separate from local service providers, making them harder
to serve. This is one challenge facing service providers in
Mexico's business centers, far away from the *maquiladoras* on the US border. Extending SEZ-type conditions to
all businesses has the added advantage of allowing them
physically to reunite. This will be increasingly important
as manufacturers continue to outsource more of their
previously in-house functions to third party service
providers.

Remove the product market barriers limiting competition in services

MGI productivity studies have shown that inappropriate product market regulations governing service sectors are the biggest
barrier to increased competition, which drives the diffusion of
more productive processes. Product market regulations govern
company ownership, trade, foreign direct investment, land use,
prices, and products. Misconceived regulations make competition
less intense by limiting the entry of new players (particularly
global ones), discouraging innovation among existing competitors, and restricting enterprise scale.[15]

- *Reduce public sector ownership.* Utilities, telecommunications, and banking remain in government hands in
  many emerging economies. Lack of investment and low
  productivity in these sectors stunt not only their own but
  also their customers' growth. According to some
  estimates, Mexico has forgone $50 billion of potential
  investment in the electricity grid because this has been
  entirely state-controlled since 1933.

- *Remove barriers to FDI in services.* This can open the door to substantial inflows of capital.[16] Moreover, it allows countries to benefit from the best practices and increased competition provided by global companies, which will impel service productivity upwards. For example, when FDI restrictions in retail banking were removed in many Latin American countries during the 1990s, foreign companies invested over $50 billion in their banking sectors alone over the next 10 years.

- *Revise unnecessary barriers to scale.* Scale can yield substantial productivity gains to enterprises. Yet many companies face limits to scale, like restrictions on store size and land use, which keep them less productive than they could be without always yielding a commensurate social gain. Productivity in housing construction, for example, depends critically on scale. Yet in Germany and France, construction companies cannot acquire lots of land big enough to support large-scale housing developments. This explains why productivity in the German and French construction industries lags far behind its equivalent in both the Netherlands and the United States.[17] Land purchase is similarly difficult in many emerging economy cities because these are large and crowded, and land titles are unclear. The solution here is to clarify titles, so land can be traded more easily and put to its most productive use.[18] Many governments also restrict store sizes to protect mom-and-pop stores from large-scale retail outlets, but at the cost of higher retail productivity. For instance, French zoning laws have required retailers to get local authorization before opening new stores bigger than 300 square meters, or expanding existing stores.[19]

Enforcement of fiscal and administrative rules to reduce informality

The high proportion of small firms in service industries makes them particularly likely to operate informally, ignoring tax requirements, employee benefits, and other regulations. This is a much larger barrier to growth than most policymakers in emerging— and developed—economies acknowledge.[20] Steps to reduce informality in local service sectors will be rewarded by rapid increases in their productivity, growth, and employment.

- *Strengthen enforcement.* Most informal businesses evade taxes and bend rules because they can get away with it. Strengthening inspection and audit services as well as increasing penalties for rule-breaking will help push enterprises into the formal sector.

- *Eliminate red tape.* So will streamlining what businesses must do to comply. For example, lots of companies never register because the process is so long and complicated. The noted economist and author Hernando de Soto found that in Egypt it takes an average of 549 days to register a new bakery.[21] Levying taxes on unregistered businesses is almost impossible, hence the importance of making registration simpler. Simplifying tax practices will compound the benefit.

- *Reduce taxes.* Many emerging economies have generous governments. But they fund their generosity by imposing high taxes on companies in the formal sector. This increases the unfair advantage enjoyed by informal players, and puts them off crossing into the formal sector. Lowering tax rates would tackle both problems. Indeed, combining lower corporate tax rates with stronger enforcement may well increase the overall tax take.

Facilitate "creative destruction" in services

Services are dynamic by nature. To maximize overall service employment, companies must be free to start up, grow, and create more jobs or—if they can't compete—to shrink, lay off workers, and close. To lubricate this process of creative destruction, governments need to make detailed policy changes.

- *Make it simpler to create and grow new firms, and close failing ones.* That means cutting the red tape surrounding both business start-ups and bankruptcies. In addition, governments should make it easier for small businesses to prove ownership of their firms. Having security of title means business owners can offer the business itself as collateral for the loans it needs to grow, and also sell it and move, when the right time comes.

- *Enhance labor mobility.* Labor laws intended to promote job security and large severance costs deter firms from taking on more people when business is brisk. Firms even try to get around such legislation by employing people as "temps" and then firing them just before the law recognizes them as permanent employees. On the other hand, restricting temporary or seasonal, or part-time employment also makes it hard for businesses to adjust staffing to fluctuations in demand. Governments should examine their labor laws for such unfortunate unintended effects, and revise them so that employers can create jobs and workers can take them more easily.

Local services have been left out of developing economy growth strategies for half a century. Import substitution, export manufacturing, and, more recently, services for export have captured policymakers' imaginations instead. But dynamic, competitive local services can unlock a huge contribution to overall GDP growth and employment. In fact, achieving higher productivity in local services is the only way for middle income—and developed—economies to ensure lifetime employment for all.

Martin Neil Baily, Diana Farrell, Jaana Remes,
McKinsey Global Institute, November 2005

Notes

1. The differences in service employment we observe among lower middle-income countries with similar levels of GDP per capita are due largely to differences in their remaining levels of agricultural employment: for example, Turkey's low share of services is explained by the fact that 46 percent of all workers are still in agriculture, while in Venezuela, only 11 percent of workers are still farming.

2. Joseph Carson, "Manufacturing Payrolls Declining Globally: The Untold Story," Alliance Capital Management, 2003.

3. OECD, "Enhancing the Performance of Service Sectors," 2005; Figure 2.14 on page 50.

4. One interviewee from the US headquarters of a leading electronics manufacturer said that of course the company accepts tax incentives, and of course its local leaders will say these are important when asked by local government representatives, but in the grand scheme of things, taxes are nevertheless very low in their priorities. The same is indicated by our survey of IT/BPO companies conducted as part of our New Horizons research. See MGI report, "New Horizons: Multinational Company Investment in Developing Economies: Policy Implications," Exhibit 4, at http://www.mckinsey.com/mgi/publications/newhorizons/index.asp.

5. G. Nicoletti and S. Scarpetta, "Regulation, Productivity and Growth," OECD economics department working paper No 347, 2003.

6. Phillppa Dee (2005), "The Economy-Wide Effects of Services Trade Barriers in Selected Developing Countries" in *Enhancing the Performance of the Services Sector,* OECD 2005.

7. See MGI report, "New Horizons: Multinational Company Investment in Developing Economies—Food Retail Case," 2003, at http://www.mckinsey.com/mgi/publications/newhorizons/index.asp.

8. See the retail sector cases of MGI's productivity reports on Thailand and Poland http://www.mckinsey.com/mgi/publications/thailand.asp and http://www.mckinsey.com/mgi/publications/poland.asp.

9. J.S. Davis and J. Haltiwanger, "Gross Job Flows" in Ashenfelter and Card (1991), *Handbook of Labor Economics*, Vol. 3, pp. 2711–2805. Our turn-over rates reported here reflect the share of jobs being destroyed and replaced by others—or half of the excess reallocation rate used in the economic literature (sum of creation and destruction rates minus the absolute value of net employment change).

10. Foster, Haltiwanger, and Krizan (1998), "Aggregate Productivity Growth: Lessons from Microeconomic Evidence" NBER Working Paper #6803.

11. Davis and Haltiwanger op. cit. cite research results from Chile and Morocco.

12. M. James Kondo, William W. Lewis, Vincent Palmade, and Yoshinori Yokoyama (Photos by Paul Van Riel), "Reviving Japan's economy," *The McKinsey Quarterly,* 2000 special edition: *Asia revalued.*

13. "Capitalism with Japanese characteristics," *The Economist,* October 6, 2005.

14. For more detail on the Brazilian food retail case, see the MGI case study at http://www.mckinsey.com/mgi/publications/newhorizons/food_retail.asp For a more general discussion of the costs arising from informality, see http://www.mckinsey.com/mgi/publications/informaleconomy.asp.

15. See Bill Lewis *The Power of Productivity: Wealth, Poverty, and the Threat to Global Stability*. University of Chicago Press, 2004.

16. For example, the FDI inflow has been a critical source for capital in the Brazil retail sector. See New Horizons food retail case op. cit.

17. See MGI Report "Removing Barriers to Growth and Employment in France and Germany" at http://www.mckinsey.com/mgi/publications/growth_barrier.asp.

18. There is, of course, a place for zoning laws. No one wants dirty factories next door to residential housing. But zoning laws are often excessively complex and restrictive. The reasonable goals of zoning can be combined with a flexible land use policy that encourages a competitive and expanding service sector.

19. See MGI Report Reaching Higher Productivity Growth in France and Germany, op cit.

20. Diana Farrell, "The Hidden Dangers of the Informal Economy," *McKinsey Quarterly* 2004 Number 3.

21. Hemando de Soto, unpublished working paper, 2003, cited in ibid.

5

Boosting government productivity

Thomas Dohrmann and Lenny T. Mendonca

IDEAS IN BRIEF

To pay for the care of the elderly, developed societies face plummeting levels of services for everyone else—and soaring taxes. Improving government productivity could greatly mitigate these problems.

In the developed world, the state commands a large share of the economy, so improving the performance of government departments can generate hundreds of billions of dollars of value.

A new focus on government productivity is needed to understand and strengthen its role in making the coming fiscal challenges more manageable and humane.

The costly retirement of 76 million US baby boomers will swell the ranks of the elderly to more than 20 percent of the population of the United States during the next 20 years. In Europe and Japan, the elderly will come to account for more than 30 percent of the population during the same period. This transformation is about to create a new sense of urgency to get the most from every government dollar. Public services beyond health care and pensions for seniors will face epic squeezes, and officials will struggle to balance the needs of retirees and younger citizens while still holding taxes to politically acceptable levels. Boosting the government's performance will be an imperative no country can ignore.

To be sure, attempts have been made before. In the United States, former Vice President Al Gore's efforts to "reinvent government" in the early 1990s scored some successes. The administration of President George W. Bush has made efforts to reform civil service rules that inhibit some sensible management practices. The Government Accountability Office (formerly the General Accounting Office) has shown perennial leadership in prodding government departments to address their management challenges. In the United Kingdom, Peter Gershon's recent review of government efficiency[1] has galvanized work to improve productivity across the public sector, with a target of £20 billion in savings by the end of 2008.

But veterans of reform efforts agree that they have barely begun to scratch the surface of the government's performance potential. One reason is that reforms take sustained attention— often rare when they become caught up in partisan or interest group politics. What's more, political cultures remain oriented to legislation, not to executing and managing programs. Few people make their name by improving the way government runs.

Nonetheless, the coming era's extraordinary fiscal pressures will force leaders to overcome these obstacles. In the developed world, the state commands a large share of the economy, so improving the performance of government departments can generate hundreds of billions of dollars of value (see "A large share"). Our experience working with public institutions in 50 countries has shown us that the opportunity, though hard to capture, is large enough to take some of the sting out of the hard choices that aging societies face. With the first baby boomers becoming eligible for retiree health and pension benefits in just a few years, there is no time to lose.

The size of the prize

Productivity lies at the heart of government performance. Although many people think that improving productivity is synonymous with cost cutting and layoffs, this misconstrues its real

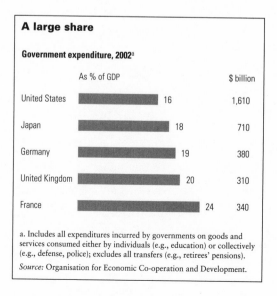

A large share

Government expenditure, 2002[a]

	As % of GDP	$ billion
United States	16	1,610
Japan	18	710
Germany	19	380
United Kingdom	20	310
France	24	340

a. Includes all expenditures incurred by governments on goods and services consumed either by individuals (e.g., education) or collectively (e.g., defense, police); excludes all transfers (e.g., retirees' pensions).

Source: Organisation for Economic Co-operation and Development.

meaning: the amount and quality of the goods and services that can be generated with a given set of inputs.

Improved productivity can certainly be achieved by reducing inputs, but it can also come from increasing the quality or quantity of the output. In fact, layoffs often lead to poorer service and thus to lower productivity; perhaps paradoxically, boosting productivity can bring both cost savings and better service.

Either way, rising productivity—whether in the public or the private sector—is the key to rising living standards. In the US semiconductor industry, for instance, productivity growth averaged 75 percent a year from 1993 to 2000 because of advances in processing speed. The price of chips stayed roughly the same, but since they were more powerful and valuable to consumers, the industry's productivity increased. In the public sector, improving educational outcomes or reducing recidivism among criminals could likewise raise productivity even if more money was spent to do so. Collecting a higher percentage of the taxes owed by people and companies would improve the productivity of tax departments.

Huge potential savings or quality improvements could come from raising government productivity, which in ten years could increase by at least 5 percent in the United States and perhaps by 15 or 20 percent—estimates that are almost certainly conservative. The potential gains in other countries are equally impressive (see "The rewards could be great").

Admittedly, estimating the public sector's productivity is problematic because some of the data are sketchy at best. From 1969 to 1994, the US Bureau of Labor Statistics (BLS) experimented with productivity measures for key government functions, only to stop because of budget cutbacks and the waning interest of policymakers. The BLS metrics used results reported

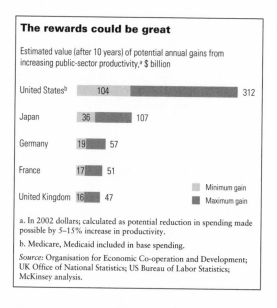

The rewards could be great

Estimated value (after 10 years) of potential annual gains from increasing public-sector productivity,[a] $ billion

United States[b]   104   312

Japan   36   107

Germany   19   57

France   17   51

United Kingdom   16   47

Minimum gain
Maximum gain

a. In 2002 dollars; calculated as potential reduction in spending made possible by 5–15% increase in productivity.
b. Medicare, Medicaid included in base spending.
Source: Organisation for Economic Co-operation and Development; UK Office of National Statistics; US Bureau of Labor Statistics; McKinsey analysis.

by government agencies and, in some areas, were not adjusted for the quality of services and value added. Yet even imperfect information offers a basis for assessing the value at stake.

To estimate the potential productivity gains, we start by comparing the productivity growth rates of the private and public sectors. For the United States, we use national-accounts data for the private sector and data from the Federal Productivity Measurement Program for the public sector. Of course, these two data sets use different selection and measurement methods, so it isn't possible to compare absolute productivity levels. But we can use the data to compare each sector's productivity growth rates and thereby to produce at least a rough estimate of the value at stake from improving government productivity.[2]

The data show that productivity in the public and private sectors rose at roughly the same pace until 1987, when a gap appeared (see "The public sector lags"). The private sector's productivity rose by 1.5 percent annually from 1987 to 1995 and by 3.0 percent annually thereafter. In contrast, our best estimates

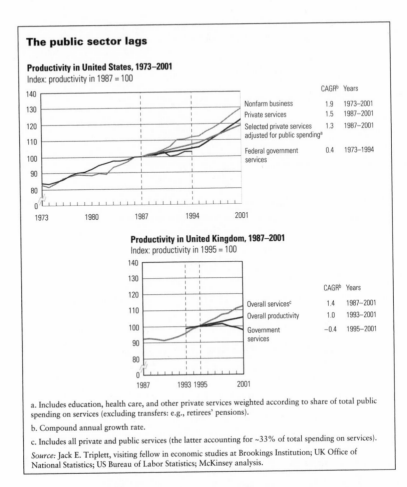

The public sector lags

Productivity in United States, 1973–2001
Index: productivity in 1987 = 100

	CAGR[b]	Years
Nonfarm business	1.9	1973–2001
Private services	1.5	1987–2001
Selected private services adjusted for public spending[a]	1.3	1987–2001
Federal government services	0.4	1973–1994

Productivity in United Kingdom, 1987–2001
Index: productivity in 1995 = 100

	CAGR[b]	Years
Overall services[c]	1.4	1987–2001
Overall productivity	1.0	1993–2001
Government services	−0.4	1995–2001

a. Includes education, health care, and other private services weighted according to share of total public spending on services (excluding transfers: e.g., retirees' pensions).

b. Compound annual growth rate.

c. Includes all private and public services (the latter accounting for ~33% of total spending on services).

Source: Jack E. Triplett, visiting fellow in economic studies at Brookings Institution; UK Office of National Statistics; US Bureau of Labor Statistics; McKinsey analysis.

show that the public sector's productivity remained almost flat, rising by just 0.4 percent from 1987 to 1994, when the BLS stopped measuring it. No evidence suggests that since then it has experienced the growth spurt enjoyed by the private sector. A similar and growing gap appears in the United Kingdom as well.[3] Data on government productivity in other countries are not available. If the US public sector could halve the estimated gap with the private sector, government productivity would be 5 to 15 percent higher in ten years, generating $104 billion to $312 billion annually.

Is it fair, though, to compare productivity growth in the public and private sectors? The economist William Baumol famously noted in 1967[4] that services may lag behind manufacturing in productivity because their labor-intensive nature makes it hard to apply cost-saving technological innovations: it will always take the same amount of time for a teacher to read a story, for instance, or for a nurse to give a shot. In this view, since the public sector largely provides services such as education, health care, and law enforcement, there is little scope for productivity improvements.

Yet Baumol's reasoning may not be as conclusive for government today as it seems. Technology is just beginning to change the nature of service delivery in health care and education fundamentally. Moreover, most government activities have direct private-sector analogs. Processing Social Security payments or tax returns resembles processing insurance claims. Managing logistics and real estate is much the same in the public and private sectors. So is procurement. Private enterprises have found ways to boost their performance substantially in each of these areas, and there is little reason to think that the public sector can't.

Our estimate of the size of the opportunity is also in line with work done by other credible researchers. John Wennberg and his colleagues at Dartmouth College, for instance, found that productivity in health care could increase by up to 25 percent.[5] Their work shows that the substantial regional variations in US Medicare costs are not associated with differences in access to health care, its quality, or health outcomes. Reducing costs in all regions to those in the lowest quintile (adjusted for differences in the prevalence of illness, medical prices, age, sex, and race) would cut annual Medicare spending by about 20 percent without affecting the recipients' standard of care.[6] Such a transformation implies a productivity increase of 25 percent. Furthermore, David Brailer, the new national coordinator for health information technology at the US Department of Health and Human Services, estimates that widespread modernization of the IT infrastructure will eventually reduce national health costs by 10 percent through administrative and clinical savings. Business Executives for National Security found that the Pentagon wastes up to 10 percent of its budget compared with more efficient private-sector organizations in functions such as housing, inventory management, payroll processing, and travel. Whatever the precise figure, all evidence points in the same direction: the opportunity to improve government productivity is huge.

Boosting the performance of government

Let us be clear: calling for a new focus on government productivity isn't meant to serve as a justification for thoughtless cuts in government spending or for "union bashing" inspired more by ideology than by a quest for effectiveness. Nor is it meant to induce complacency in the face of the hard budget choices that aging societies will face.

Instead, our call to action is meant to promote a necessary conversation on the role that government productivity can play in making the coming fiscal challenges more manageable and humane. In an era of permanent fiscal pressure, liberals should welcome a more efficient government to assure that more money is available for social needs. Conservatives should welcome it to help keep taxes at levels consistent with strong economic growth. Rightly understood, better performance by government can become that rare arena in which common ground is possible.

Over the past decade, a handful of public-sector organizations around the world—schools, public-welfare agencies, health care systems, postal and transit systems, and militaries—have improved their performance by 5 to 30 percent or more. Often they have chosen among three classic management tools to raise productivity: organizational redesign, strategic procurement, and operational redesign. In the most effective cases, these tools were part of a broader program of cultural change that transformed the organization's performance and measured it rigorously.[7]

Organizational redesign

A redesign that focuses on the end "customer," eliminates duplication, and streamlines processes that can improve both the cost and the quality of services. Consider the experience of the US state of Illinois. In 1997 it put public-aid programs from six separate departments under a single roof. Previously it had been necessary to approach each of them separately and to give them the same information, even though more than half of their 1.8 million customers received more than one service. The new Department of Human Services is a one-stop shop ensuring that recipients get all of the services they need—in the past many of them hadn't—and eliminating the duplication of programs and back-office processes. As a result, the department has redeployed money and staff to new programs, such as an early-intervention initiative.

The German Federal Employment Agency (Bundesagentur für Arbeit) is also reorganizing, amid a controversial and often bitter public debate about the future course of German social and labor policy. Headquarters have been shrunk down to 400 staff members, from 1,100, and operational responsibilities have in effect been decentralized to ten regional divisions. The radical redesign of local agencies and their service offerings has been successfully prototyped and now gives customers tangible benefits, such as halving waiting times and doubling the amount of time available for counseling. These changes have led to much higher customer satisfaction levels.

Procurement

Improving supplier-management and purchasing operations can help organizations cut their expenditures while raising the quality of the goods and services they buy. Governments mounting such efforts usually standardize and consolidate orders, designate preferred suppliers, reward them for meeting delivery and quality targets, and collaborate with them on ways to improve production processes and reduce costs. Government regulations sometimes make revamping public-sector procurement difficult, but enormous progress can still be made: Illinois saved more than $100 million in fiscal year 2004 and expects to save more than $200 million in fiscal year 2005 (see "How Illinois cut its purchasing bills"). For many items, the state is getting better quality.

Sometimes procurement officials cut costs dramatically by understanding the suppliers' economics. A US federal agency, for example, recently renewed an IT contract with outside vendors. By building a detailed model of the suppliers' costs and benchmarking their individual components, it negotiated prices that were more than 60 percent lower than the first set of competitive bids it received and will save several hundred million dollars over the term of a five-year deal.

These are not unique opportunities: Most government agencies could improve their procurement processes. The state of Tennessee, for instance, is projected to save more than $300 million annually in Medicare and Medicaid costs, without any changes in health outcomes, by purchasing the cheapest drugs available rather than name-brand ones. Schools throughout the United States have saved 10 to 35 percent on food, janitorial services, textbooks, and transportation by purchasing them more astutely. (Large school systems can save $30 million to $40 million a year in this way.) Military and security spending is an even bigger opportunity, in part because it accounts for more than 70 percent of total government contracting. The United Kingdom is trying to capture this opportunity through its Smart Acquisition program, a set of reforms designed to reduce bureaucracy, cut procurement costs, and speed up the delivery of equipment.

Operational redesign

Redesigning operational processes to reduce waste, eliminate unneeded effort, and correct mistakes quickly can also raise productivity to an astonishing extent. Consider the experience of the United States Postal Service (USPS). Since 1999, the number of addresses it serves has increased by 7 million—nearly equivalent to the number of addresses in the entire Chicago metropolitan area. Nonetheless, the USPS has saved $5.5 billion by replicating the best practices of the best sorting plants and by improving its delivery and counter operations. In this way, it cut its full-time workforce to 69,000, mainly through retirement and normal attrition, and increased its productivity by 6 percent.

Customer satisfaction ratings and other service-quality metrics are at all-time highs (see "You have mail, efficiently").

"E-government" initiatives too can radically improve service and customer satisfaction while reducing costs by 25 percent or more.[8] In Singapore, an export license that formerly required 21 forms and took three weeks to process now involves one online application that can be approved in 15 seconds. The US Internal Revenue Service can process an online tax return for just $0.40, compared with $1.60 for a paper return, and the Arizona Department of Transportation can renew a driver's license online for $1.60, compared with $6.60 at a branch office. Combining online delivery with a redesign of the back-office processes supporting it can realize cost savings of 35 to 40 percent—while customer satisfaction soars.

Overcoming the barriers

If governments could improve their performance easily, they would have done so already. In fact, they face unusual challenges. Competition is the most important missing element. More than a decade of McKinsey Global Institute research around the world shows that monopolies, businesses protected by government regulation, and other private-sector companies without competitors nearly always have very low productivity.[9] Without competition, managers have little incentive to take risks on new techniques.

For governments, the solution is creating competition to provide services and giving citizens the ability to choose among these alternatives. Charter schools, for example, create competition in public education. Outsourcing back-office services such as procurement, real-estate management, and payrolls and benefits creates competition in these functions. Allowing private-sector companies to bid on social-service contracts lets them compete with government providers.

A part of the answer for aging populations?

If sustained growth in public-sector productivity began now, it could contribute to some easing of the looming fiscal crisis that will accompany the rapid aging of the populations of developed countries. The Organisation for Economic Co-operation and Development (OECD) estimates that by 2050 public expenditures will have increased by an average of 6 percent of GDP to accommodate the needs of retirees.[a] But the Center for Strategic and International Studies (CSIS) argues that these projections are too optimistic and that increases in spending could amount to more than 12 percent of GDP by 2040.[b] Using assumptions lying somewhere between those of the OECD and the CSIS, we estimate that spending will increase by 8 percent of GDP in the United States, where higher birth and immigration rates are expected to make the impact of aging less dramatic than it will be in other advanced countries, and by more than 10 percent of GDP in Germany, where the aging trend is more pronounced.

The usual options for controlling the massive expenditures that will soon be needed to accommodate the elderly are reducing the level or growth of government benefits for them, cutting public services for the rest of the population, and raising taxes. Enhancing public-sector productivity could make any of these options less painful. In fact, raising it by an extra 1.4 percent a year in the United States and by an extra 1.6 percent in Germany would let their governments sustain current levels of public services and social-welfare benefits, without additional taxes or borrowing.

These are undoubtedly very large improvements, but they might be possible. After all, from 1987 to 1994 the private sector's productivity growth rate in the United States was 1.0 percent higher than the best estimate for that of the public sector. In the United Kingdom it was 1.8 percent higher from 1995 to 2001. Even if reducing the gap doesn't eliminate the fiscal impact of aging populations on its own, it could take some of the sting out of the hard fiscal choices societies will face coping with them.

a. Pablo Antolin, Thai-Thanh Dang, and Howard Oxley, *Fiscal Implications of Ageing: Projections of Age-Related Spending,* OECD Economics Department working paper number 305 (2001).

b. Neil Howe and Richard Jackson, *The 2003 Aging Vulnerability Index,* Center for Strategic and International Studies and Watson Wyatt Worldwide, Washington, DC, 2003; and Richard Jackson, *The Global Retirement Crisis,* Center for Strategic and International Studies and Citigroup, Washington, DC, 2002. Both papers can be found at www.csis.org.

When creating competition in the public sector isn't possible, its leaders can devise other incentives. For one thing, managers can be prodded to meet targets if governments budget in expected performance improvements; in the United Kingdom, the Gershon review of the public sector's efficiency has given each government department three-year productivity targets covering financial savings and head count reductions while at the same time ensuring that services will continue to be provided. Making the performance of governments more transparent by publishing the results of customer satisfaction surveys, benchmarking surveys, and service-quality metrics also helps citizens to take an active role in demanding change.

If the execution challenges are daunting, the principles and prerequisites for success are clear. When public-sector operations become more transparent, accountability increases. Benchmarking and tracking performance help managers to raise their game. Exposing activities to competition improves service and cuts costs. The keys are committed leadership, a critical mass of talent, processes that budget for productivity targets, and citizens who know that they have a stake in a better outcome and hold officials accountable for achieving it. One way of building public confidence and media support and of stoking the appetite for change is to design the reform effort so that it delivers high-profile early victories.

If not now, when?

Given the magnitude of the opportunity, there are only two paths forward. The first—government as usual—ensures that in the decades ahead citizens will pay higher taxes and receive fewer, lower-quality services while financing the baby boomers' retirement. Public alienation seems likely to deepen just when governments already face a talent crisis as a generation of managers heads toward retirement.

The other path—developing a serious and sustained agenda to boost performance throughout the government—won't be easy. But as part of a broad national effort to meet the challenge of an aging population, it could draw new talent to public service at a crucial moment. Today governments at all levels face an unprecedented loss of talent and institutional knowledge. Nearly three-quarters of all senior federal executives could retire in the next few years; in California, nearly a third of the state's entire workforce could. To inspire a new generation capable of filling the shoes of these retiring leaders, government must transform itself.

If leaders of governments started to think differently about how they do and could work, the results would surprise the cynics. The public sector, after all, guided some of history's most extraordinary management feats, from the Manhattan Project to space flight to bullet trains to smallpox eradication. An agenda to revitalize government could make citizens more engaged with it, initiate a virtuous cycle of continual improvement, and ease the impact of an aging society (see "A part of the answer for aging populations?").

Even without a broad mandate, visionary government executives can begin making real progress on productivity in their own organizations. The leaders of the German Federal Employment Agency, Illinois, and the USPS have shown the enormous gains that can be made. By starting with less politically charged areas, such as procurement, government leaders can gain the experience and credibility to tackle more sensitive ones, including education and health care.

Unprecedented fiscal pressures that are only a few years away should promote a new kind of national conversation, in which shibboleths can be rethought. Leaders at all levels of government must consider how their own organizations can immediately start to plan and implement the performance improvements that advanced nations will desperately need. The time for action is now.

The authors wish to thank Paul Callan, Diana Farrell, and Pamela Keenan Fritz for their thoughtful input into this article.

How Illinois cut its purchasing bills

Chip W. Hardt and Ravi P. Rao

With huge swaths of the labor market set to retire in the coming years, the public sector will soon face intensifying pressure to top up its coffers in order to provide services for aging citizens. More people living on fixed incomes mean that state governments can't rely on the personal income tax and other traditional revenue boosters to fill budget gaps. Alternative revenue generators, including casinos and lotteries, are already showing their limitations.

To stanch the red ink, it will be necessary to take a hard look at the other side of the equation: cost-management and procurement policies. Increasingly, governments will have to borrow best practices from the private sector and alter them to suit agencies that often not only don't enjoy the degree of managerial freedom that prevails there but also face strong resistance by employees to change. Such obstacles may have prevented the earlier adoption of private-sector practices, even as the dot-com bust and the economic downturn of 2001 upended the budgets of states, local governments, and school districts, making more efficient management necessary.

Purchasing is one area in which states can innovate successfully despite these barriers. Last year, Illinois transformed its procurement system, a patchwork of agencies stitched together over the past 175 years. In the process, it saved roughly $110 million out of the $15 billion spent each year on goods and services, such as prison food, phone calls, and copy machines. For fiscal year 2005, the state is on track to save twice as much.

The way Illinois achieved these savings provides lessons for other state governments. By the time it began its transformation process, in 2003, it had become a conglomerate of more than 100 agencies, departments, and commissions, which in all spend more than $50 billion a year. If the state were a private-sector business, "Illinois Inc." would rank in the Fortune 100. Each agency or department has its own budget and determines its own spending needs—the notion being that the missions and corresponding strategies and operations of different agencies vary greatly, so they require as much flexibility as possible. The state's decentralized model, however, creates some predictable difficulties, such as the signing of a number of contracts for the same items and a failure to leverage the state's purchasing power or to share learning across agencies. A "silo mentality" reinforces these difficulties. The all-too-familiar results are financial deficits, poor service levels, project delays, budget overruns, and low organizational morale.

Illinois set out to transform its purchasing culture by promoting a new, centrally led, One State model to help it procure goods and services as a single entity. Hundreds of employees throughout the state helped plan new purchasing strategies and in the process gained training in the new approach.

Amid these efforts to shake up the state's purchasing culture, Illinois designed a two-pronged effort to drive down spending. The first was a "quick-sourcing" initiative that used benchmarked prices as a tool to renegotiate contracts with vendors. The second was a total-cost-of-ownership (TCO) approach focusing on two major spending questions—what to buy and how to buy it—which help determine all of the long-term cost elements of an item and all of the drivers of those costs.

Quick sourcing relies on the premise that vendors will renegotiate their contracts in the state's favor when confronted with benchmarking data showing that they may have overcharged for goods or services in the past. It helped Illinois to identify $30 million in annual savings, including $3 million a year for telephone bills alone. The benchmarking information has been included in a new online database, so that future negotiators—no matter what their agency, department, or commission—can take advantage of the work already completed.

In addition to the price cuts earned through quick sourcing, Illinois deployed TCO methods to find an additional $80 million in savings during the initiative's first year. By focusing on what to buy, for example, the state Department of Corrections saved $2 million a year on prison food, in part by eliminating costly items (such as tuna and grapefruit) from the menu and replacing them with less expensive but comparable items, such as ground beef and oranges. In most cases, the challenge came in convincing officials that the substitutions and cuts wouldn't result in inferior services.

After looking at how to buy—the other major aspect of the state's TCO approach—a team from a number of agencies recommended, among other things, that Illinois attempt to consolidate all of its contracts for temporary services. The decentralized hiring of clerical workers had been an attempt to accommodate the divergent needs of different agencies but meant that the state had not been able to leverage its size to get better prices. By combining contracts, it saved $2 million during the first year. In this case, changing how the state bought services involved coordinating the needs of agencies that had rarely collaborated in the past. The change also posed a new political challenge: fewer contracts mean that the state has fewer opportunities to expand the amount of business it does with companies owned by members of minority groups and by women.

The experience of Illinois shows that state and local governments adopting best purchasing practices can achieve big savings. Clearly, however, for these procurement approaches to succeed, states must transform their cultural DNA.

You have mail, efficiently

Thomas Dohrmann and Stephen K. Sacks

Ever since Henry Ford came up with his revolutionary assembly line, manufacturing companies have constantly sought to raise their efficiency by redesigning operations. More recently, public-sector organizations have found that they too can boost productivity by reducing waste, eliminating unneeded effort, correcting mistakes quickly, and encouraging workers to suggest ideas for improvement.

A variety of challenges inspired the United States Postal Service to begin considering such an operational redesign in 1999. The number of addresses the USPS served was growing by 1.8 million every year, without corresponding increases in the revenue it generated or in mail volumes, which were projected to stop growing or even decline. Like many public-sector organizations, it faced regulations that, combined with its powerful labor unions, made it nearly impossible to close plants or to lay off workers. Moreover, largely as a result of having prices pegged to costs by the government, the USPS had developed a culture in which managers were rarely expected to improve productivity. In this environment, merely maintaining service levels and raising the price of stamps by rates at (or even below) the inflation rate counted as a success. Productivity had therefore been essentially flat for ten years, growing at only 0.2 percent annually, compared with the 3 to 5 percent expected in the private sector.

An initial analysis of the problems indicated that the best mail-sorting plants and delivery units were twice as productive as the least productive ones—and that potential opportunities to improve productivity were substantial. To pursue them, the postal service's leadership decided to launch what it called a "breakthrough productivity initiative."

A team of 15 people handpicked by senior management led the charge. The first finding was that performance data were murky at best: it was hard to tell with any real precision how well plants and delivery operations were performing or to compare performance across plants or delivery units. To remedy this problem, the team decided that detailed performance data should be captured by an information system and distributed through an intranet site where USPS employees could monitor the performance of every plant and delivery unit. Grouping all of the plants into seven categories, each with similar characteristics (such as size or layout), provided for meaningful comparisons.

First, the team used the data to set improvement targets for each plant and delivery unit and to lock them into budgets. While there was resistance initially, the organization began to accept the new approach after a few budget cycles, and managers soon came to expect that they would be asked to increase productivity each year. A new incentive and recognition system rewards those who do. Second, to help managers meet their budget targets, the team used the data to reveal best practices throughout the organization. A sorting plant in New York City, for example, processed only 5 percent of its total mail by hand, versus a nationwide rate of 10 percent. The approach of the New York plant was simple: its workers quickly looked through mail containers destined for manual sorting and decided which of them could go onto its automated equipment. When the USPS applied this practice across all plants, it generated several hundred million dollars a year in cost savings, since manual sorting is actually ten times more expensive than automated sorting.

After the productivity improvements kicked in, a simple scheduling tool revealed that the USPS had more workers than it needed overall, even at peak times. The team therefore suggested ways of matching the organization's staff levels to its variable workloads. Nonetheless, throughout the whole labor-reduction process, the USPS leadership fully cooperated with the unions, avoiding layoffs entirely. Natural attrition, the use of fewer temps, and less overtime for some workers cut full-time employment levels by 15 percent, thereby creating a much leaner organization.

Although the breakthrough productivity team finds and dissemi- nates best practices across the organization, the nine area vice presidents across the country are ultimately responsible for deciding how to meet their productivity targets. As this kind of accountability has taken hold across the organization's 380 mail-sorting plants and

27,000 delivery units, it has reduced the variability of performance among branches, standardized processes, and spread best practices to the worst performers. These achievements have in turn decreased the USPS operating budget by more than $5.5 billion—close to 10 percent—in four years' time.

Thomas Dohrmann and Lenny T. Mendonca,
McKinsey Quarterly, 2004 Number 4.

Notes

1. Peter Gershon, *Releasing Resources to the Front Line: Independent Review of Public Sector Efficiency,* July 2004 (www.hm-treasury .gov.uk).

2. For a full description of the challenges of comparing the two data sets, see Donald Fisk and Darlene Forte, "The Federal Productivity Measurement Program: Final results," *Monthly Labor Review,* 1997, Volume 120, Number 5, pp. 19–28.

3. The UK Office of National Statistics is revising its metrics, and the public-sector productivity numbers may rise, although there are no indications that they would equal or surpass those of the private sector.

4. William J. Baumol, "Macroeconomics of unbalanced growth: The anatomy of urban crisis," *American Economic Review,* Volume 57, Number 3, pp. 415–426.

5. Elliott S. Fisher, Daniel J. Gottlieb, F. L. Lucas, Étoile L. Pinder, Thérèse A. Stukel, and David E. Wennberg, "The implications of regional variations in Medicare spending," *Annals of Internal Medicine,* 2003, Volume 138, Issue 4, pp. 273–287. John Wennberg, the director of the Center for the Evaluative Clinical Sciences, at Dartmouth Medical School, pioneered research into regional Medicare patterns. The paper cited in this footnote has David Wennberg, another researcher, as one of its authors.

6. Elliott Fisher and Jonathan Skinner, "Regional disparities in Medicare expenditures: An opportunity for reform," *National Tax Journal,* 1997, Volume 50, Number 3, pp. 413–425.

7. Emily Lawson and Colin Price, "The psychology of change management," *The McKinsey Quarterly,* 2003 special edition: The value in organization, pp. 30–41 (www.mckinseyquarterly.com/links/ 14579); Jennifer A. LaClair and Ravi P. Rao, "Helping employees embrace change," *The McKinsey Quarterly,* 2002 Number 4, pp. 17–20 (www.mckinseyquarterly.com/links/14581); and Jonathan D. Day and

Michael Jung, "Corporate transformation without a crisis," *The McKinsey Quarterly,* 2000 Number 4, pp. 116–127 (www.mckinseyquarterly.com/links/14583).

8. Gassan Al-Kibsi, Kito de Boer, Mona Mourshed, and Nigel P. Rea, "Putting citizens on-line, not in line," *The McKinsey Quarterly,* 2001 special edition: *On-line tactics,* pp. 64–73 (www.mckinseyquarterly.com/links/14585).

9. William W. Lewis, "The power of productivity," *The McKinsey Quarterly,* 2004 Number 2, pp. 100–111 (www.mckinseyquarterly.com/links/14587).

6

Beyond cheap labor: lessons for developing economies

Diana Farrell, Antonio Puron, and Jaana K. Remes

IDEAS IN BRIEF

China's economic surge and its entry into the World Trade Organization have sparked alarm across the developing world and in middle-income countries such as Brazil, Mexico, Poland, Portugal, and South Korea.

Rather than trying to win back low-wage jobs from China, developing countries should transition to higher-value-added activities and push forward with reforms.

To earn higher wages in a globalized economy, middle-income nations must find and exploit their competitive advantages.

Buoyed by the North American Free Trade Agreement (NAFTA), Mexico in the 1990s was the bustling factory floor of the Americas. But since 2000, as China rose to assume that role, more than 270,000 Mexicans have lost assembly jobs, hundreds of factories have closed their doors, and Mexico's trade deficit with China has grown to more than $5 billion. The ubiquitous "Made in China" stamp, found on everything from toys to textiles to statues of Our Lady of Guadalupe, has become the incarnation of the single greatest perceived threat to Mexico's economic prosperity—and a symbol of the pitfalls of globalization.

Mexico's fears are not unique. China's economic surge and its entry into the World Trade Organization have sparked alarm across the developing world. In middle-income countries such as Brazil, Poland, Portugal, and South Korea, a rising standard of living makes their position as low-wage producers and exporters increasingly tenuous.

Rather than fixating on jobs lost to China, these countries should remember a fact of economic life: no place can remain the world's low-cost producer forever—even China will lose that title one day. Instead of trying to defend low-wage assembly jobs, Mexico and other middle-income countries should focus on creating jobs that add higher value. Only if more productive companies with higher-value-added activities replace less productive ones can middle-income economies continue down the development path. Even so, being part of the global economy requires these countries, like Lewis Carroll's Alice in *Through the Looking Glass,* to do a lot of running just to stay in the same place. Unfortunately, for too many of them the focus on China—and, more broadly, political rhetoric against globalization—are blocking reform efforts.

Blame China?

To developing countries watching foreign investors head east, China's economic prowess might seem invincible, but history suggests otherwise. Only 20 years ago, for example, the United States was convinced that the superior business models and industrial policies of Germany and Japan would shutter every last domestic factory door. In the 1990s, the United States fretted about the threat from the high-tech industries of South Korea and Taiwan, while presidential candidates warned of the "giant sucking sound" made by the migration of jobs to Mexico under NAFTA. These days, the United States is more concerned about the effect of China's economy on its trade balance and employment rate. But the rate of unemployment in the United States today is lower than it was 20 years ago.

Nearly all countries worry about jobs lost to others—a fact often exploited for political ends. The demagoguery obscures the fact that countries can and do continually evolve to meet the challenges presented by new competitors outside their borders.

Mexico is a case in point. Like most middle-income countries, it has grown more prosperous through freer trade and liberalization. Its average household income is now more than twice the level in China and other low-wage countries, and its manufacturing wage rates reflect this increasing prosperity (see "Mexico moves on up"). But the *maquiladora* assembly operations that line the US border—often the most visible face of Mexico's entry into the global economy—make only a small contribution to

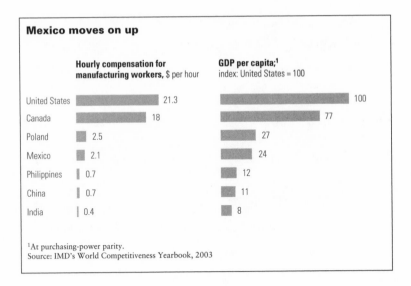

Mexico moves on up

	Hourly compensation for manufacturing workers, $ per hour	GDP per capita;[1] index: United States = 100
United States	21.3	100
Canada	18	77
Poland	2.5	27
Mexico	2.1	24
Philippines	0.7	12
China	0.7	11
India	0.4	8

[1] At purchasing-power parity.
Source: IMD's World Competitiveness Yearbook, 2003

this rising prosperity. Since NAFTA came into effect, in 1994, the country has received upward of $170 billion in foreign direct investment—more than three times the amount that India attracted. Yet less than 15 percent of this investment has gone to the *maquiladoras* (see "Bumping along the bottom"); the vast majority has been motivated by a desire to produce goods and services to sell into Mexico's large domestic market, not to produce cheap goods for export. Our research shows that non-*maquiladora* investments have generated a wide range of benefits for Mexico's economy by creating jobs, boosting competition and productivity, lowering prices, and enhancing consumer choice.[3] Consider the impact of foreign investment on Mexico's automobile market: consumers can now choose from dozens of models, compared with just a few of them before. In the retailing industry, the price of fresh food in Mexico City is 40 percent below its level in 1993, the year before NAFTA opened up the economy. The lesson for Mexico and for other countries where jobs are going offshore is this: don't overestimate the value of low-wage employment to your economy's prospects.

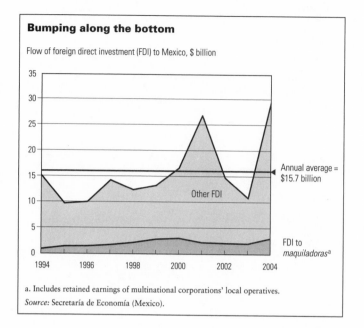

Bumping along the bottom

Flow of foreign direct investment (FDI) to Mexico, $ billion

Annual average = $15.7 billion

Other FDI

FDI to maquiladoras[a]

a. Includes retained earnings of multinational corporations' local operatives.

Source: Secretaría de Economía (Mexico).

Furthermore, even if these jobs were worth protecting, it would not make sense for Mexico to see China as the source of its woes. El Salvador, Guatemala, and Honduras have wage rates just 25 to 40 percent of Mexico's and offer almost the same advantages of proximity. Economists at the Federal Reserve Bank of Dallas have shown that increases in Mexico's wage costs relative to these non-Chinese competitors and the decline in US industrial production together account for 80 percent of the *maquiladora*[3] jobs lost since their peak in 2000.[4]

Jobs in offshore assembly operations are essentially unstable because they are exceedingly sensitive to changes in the global business cycle, since multinational companies tend to adjust production volumes abroad before doing so at home. Foreign investment thus poured into Mexico during the boom years of the late 1990s but then dropped with the US downturn of 2001–2002. Just as predictably, Mexican assembly operations started to grow again in 2004 as US demand picked up. In the

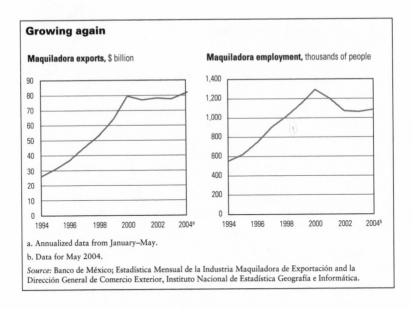

Growing again

Maquiladora exports, $ billion

Maquiladora employment, thousands of people

a. Annualized data from January–May.

b. Data for May 2004.

Source: Banco de México; Estadística Mensual de la Industria Maquiladora de Exportación and la Dirección General de Comercio Exterior, Instituto Nacional de Estadística Geografía e Informática.

first five months of the year, *maquiladora* exports rose by more than 20 percent and employment turned to growth as well (see "Growing again"). But Mexico shouldn't be content with this recovery in unstable jobs; policymakers still need to push reforms that will move the country up the economic ladder, to secure better-quality employment for more people, and higher growth overall.

The road to adding higher value

Rather than try to win back low-wage, low-skill assembly jobs, middle-income countries should undertake three essential steps to further their economic development. They must encourage the transition to higher-value-added activities, identify and exploit their comparative advantage, and push forward with reforms that create more competition, entrepreneurship, and flexibility.

Encouraging the transition

The experience of developed countries suggests that expansion into higher-value-added activities comes not from a shift into entirely new industries, such as high tech, biotech, or nanotech, but from the natural evolution of companies within existing industries.

As countries around the world develop, a similar series of events has played out: companies start out in the simple, labor-intensive parts of an industry but over time hone their skills to compete in more profitable areas, such as marketing, product design, and the manufacture of sophisticated intermediate inputs. In northern Italy's textile and apparel industry, for example, the majority of garment production has moved to lower-cost locations, but employment remains stable because companies have put more resources into tasks such as designing clothes and coordinating global production networks. In the US automotive industry, imports of finished cars from Mexico increased rapidly after NAFTA took effect, but exports of US auto parts to it have quadrupled, allowing much of the more capital-intensive work—and many of the higher-paid jobs—to remain in the United States.

Unfortunately, governments in both developing and developed countries often do a poor job of encouraging the transition to higher-value-adding activities. In the United States, for instance, the offshore assembly program (OAP) requires goods produced abroad to use a certain percentage of US components (typically 80 percent) to qualify for reduced tariffs. Since this stipulation is the basis of the maquiladora regime itself, Mexico allows foreign companies to import machinery, raw materials, and parts duty-free if the final products are exported. But as a result, imported inputs represent 76 percent of these goods' total export value, and most of the rest is labor; locally produced intermediate inputs represent less than 2 percent of production value. Moreover, while allowing foreign competitors into the export segments, the government of Mexico sheltered the rest of its economy from the benefits of global competition. Today fewer than 50 companies, most of them foreign, dominate Mexican exports—Petróleos Mexicanos (Pemex) being the main exception.

Furthermore, many countries unintentionally hamper the transition to higher-value-added activities by adopting regulations that aim to create positive spillover effects from foreign investment in local industry, but have negative results instead. Mexico, for instance, instituted local-content requirements in the automotive and consumer electronics industries when it first opened these sectors up to foreign investment; it also capped foreign ownership in the latter. Yet in almost all cases, these policies failed to spark the development of strong local suppliers or domestic companies; they have merely served to create a protective umbrella for the supplier sectors, which therefore don't flourish. In these industries, Mexico's experience mirrors that of Brazil, China, and India.[5]

Exploiting a comparative advantage

To justify higher wages in a globalized economy, middle-income nations must find and develop their comparative advantage. The former Eastern Bloc countries, for instance, have highly educated, moderately paid scientists and engineers and are therefore a natural offshoring base for Western European companies.[6] India's well-educated, English-speaking workforce gives it a comparative advantage in information technology and business outsourcing. Members of the Association of South East Asian Nations

(ASEAN) have a common market the size of Europe and thus offer foreign investors not just a low-wage export base but also a huge domestic market. Brazil and India too have the advantage of market size.

Fortunately, Mexico also has a unique advantage: it sits next to the world's largest consumer market. Some Mexicans may see that as a political or social liability, yet the country is an ideal location for designing and producing items for which proximity to the end user matters.

Proximity is important for many reasons. Some goods, such as large-screen TVs and white goods, have high transportation costs.[7] A very different example is the almost $4 billion market for the plastic bottle caps that seal most of the soft-drink and water bottles sold in the United States. They may be small and light, but their aggregate bulk means they also have high shipping costs, so it is more economical to produce them close to the United States.

Time sensitivity is another consideration. Fresh food can spoil, and fashionable items or promotional materials can miss their window of relevance.[8] In a fast-evolving market, goods such as computers have slim margins and depreciate rapidly in value after production. This factor helps explain why many of the PCs sold in the United States are assembled in North America, though most of the components are produced in Asia.

Products that require extensive interaction among different players in the value chain also benefit from proximity. Sales of customized products—from personal computers to tailor-made clothing to look-alike bobble-head dolls—are expanding rapidly thanks to the online channel.

What's more, lean retailing in the United States demands shorter delivery times for a wider range of products, since suppliers must replenish their stock more frequently in response to changes in sales and inventory volumes. This factor, combined with the growing number of consumer goods that retailers offer, means that many suppliers face an exponential increase in the complexity of their logistics. Consider the Lands' End pinpoint cotton Oxford dress shirt, which offers the usual choices of neck and sleeve length, five different collar types, and two cuts. Even if the shirt were available to consumers in only blue and white, that still generates hundreds of possible combinations. Add other fabrics, colors, and patterns, and this simple shirt quickly goes into the tens of thousands of SKUs (stock-keeping units). As a result, the optimal strategy for most apparel makers is to split production between nearby locations and lowest-cost countries. Thus Mexico's share of time-sensitive goods like jeans for teenagers increased during the 1990s, while China's production of commodity items such as knit pullovers has also grown.[9]

Push reform

As low-skill, labor-intensive operations head elsewhere, middle-income countries may try to lure them back with tax breaks and other financial incentives. They should resist this temptation. Such initiatives are not likely to influence foreign investment significantly and won't compensate for rising wage rates over the longer term. Enticements of this sort merely divert resources from the government and society to multinational companies. In some cases they can lead to counterproductive overinvestment. In Brazil's auto sector, foreign carmakers responded to subsidies worth more than $100,000 for each new job by adding many more workers—and saddling the industry with 80 percent overcapacity a few years later.[10]

Instead of spending tax money to offer financial incentives to foreign investors, governments should use the funds to improve transportation networks, power grids, and telecommunications lines. Beyond that, policymakers must boost competition in the broader economy so that companies are compelled to improve their operations, adopt best practices, innovate, and move up the economic value chain. Too often, developing countries concentrate on special economic zones or preferred export industries while competition languishes in the remaining sectors. Price controls, tariffs, licensing requirements, and other product regulations limit market entry and reduce competition.

As India's $5 billion auto industry demonstrates, the gains from removing these stifling regulations can be dramatic. Twenty years ago, two state-owned carmakers—Hindustan Motors and Premier Automobiles Limited (PAL)—dominated the market and offered just a handful of outdated models. In 1983 the government allowed Suzuki Motor to take a minority stake in a joint venture with the small state-owned automaker Maruti Udyog, and in 1992 nine more foreign automakers were allowed to invest in India. This infusion of new capital and technology created serious competition for the two incumbents, eventually forcing PAL out. The industry, one of the fastest growing in the world, now produces 13 times more cars than it did 20 years ago. Tata Motors hit a milestone in 2004 by exporting 20,000 cars to the United Kingdom. Meanwhile, prices for consumers in India have fallen by 8 to 10 percent annually, unleashing a burst of demand and allowing steady employment despite rapidly rising productivity.

The reform agenda for each middle-income country will vary. In Brazil, for example, a major obstacle to growth is the informal economy, which consists of businesses that fail to comply with tax and regulatory obligations. The World Bank estimates that this gray sector employs 55 percent of all labor in Brazil and shows no sign of diminishing: according to our research, it has grown rapidly in some industries, such as construction. The unearned cost advantage that informal businesses enjoy allows them to undercut the prices of more productive competitors and stay in business despite very low productivity. (see "The hidden dangers of the informal economy" in this volume) Butchers, for instance, can save nearly 30 percent of their costs by skirting hygiene and quality standards. Modern supermarkets have found that acquiring informal grocers is unprofitable once value-added and labor taxes are paid. The informal economy thus distorts competition and disrupts the natural evolution in which more productive companies replace less productive ones. We estimate that if Brazil reduced the size of its informal economy by 20 percent, GDP growth would increase by as much as 1.5 percent annually (see "Reining in Brazil's economy" in this volume). The potential benefits to Portugal and Turkey are similar.

In Mexico's case, the main barriers to movement up the economic value chain are a thicket of burdensome regulations and an inadequate infrastructure. According to a World Bank report,[11] it takes an average of 58 days to start a business in Mexico, compared with 8 in Singapore and 9 in Turkey. It takes 74 days to register a property in Mexico but only 12 in the United States. Enforcing a contract requires 37 different procedures and takes 421 days to wind through the legal system, while closing an insolvent business can drag on for more than a year and a half. Moreover, Mexico's corporate-income-tax rate of 34 percent is twice as high as China's. These problems not only discourage foreign investment but also stifle local entrepreneurship and the growth of domestic companies.

Since capital-intensive production is highly sensitive to factor costs, Mexico must invest in infrastructure. Electricity costs in Mexico are, on average, 10 percent higher than US levels, for example, and more than 40 percent above China's. By some estimates, the country should invest $50 billion to upgrade its power grid. Mexico's telecommunications network is equally lamentable—a prime reason the country isn't a more prominent location for offshore operations serving Spanish-speaking customers. Mexico's ground, air, and sea transportation systems all need improvement to build on its advantage of proximity to the United States.

Development: One company at a time

Although government reform can create the conditions for economic development, individual companies must act as catalysts for change within their industry, as can individual executives. For example, plant managers assess their immediate competitive environment and react by improving their operations.

US semiconductor players, for instance, responded to competition from Japanese companies in the late 1980s. Japan quickly became dominant in sectors such as memory chips, spurring a public outcry in the United States over unfair competition and the loss of high-paying white-collar jobs. But US chip makers reinvented themselves. The big players—Intel, Motorola, and Texas Instruments—abandoned the dynamic-random-access-memory (DRAM) business and then invested more heavily in the manufacture of microprocessors and logic products, the next wave of growth in semiconductors. Intel became an even more significant global force in microprocessors, while TI became a dominant player in digital signal processors (the "brain" in mobile telephones). Motorola gained a strong position in microcontrollers and automotive semiconductors. Throughout this shift toward higher-value-added activities, the total number of US jobs in semiconductors and closely related electronics fields held constant at around half a million.[12]

The experience of a handful of Mexican companies has already shown that they too can compete by shifting their production to more advanced and lucrative goods for the North American marketplace. Their success should provide a dose of optimism for their compatriots as well as for businesses in other middle-income nations anxiously watching cost advantages erode.

One such company is Jabil Circuit, a contract manufacturer of electronics products for the likes of Dell and Nokia. Few Mexican industries have been hit harder over the past few years than electronics. As orders were lost to Asia, Jabil saw its workforce of 3,500 shrink by half from 2001 to 2002.[13] Instead of trying to win back lost orders, it learned to make more complex and customized products (computer routers and handheld credit-card machines, for example) that were traditionally made in the United States.

Managers at one of the company's Mexican plants very deliberately studied the US market to ascertain the necessary performance levels and the areas in which lower-cost labor could create an advantage. As a result, the factory retooled its inventory system and trained workers to undertake more than one task at a time, so the number of items it was able to produce rose to more than 6,000, from 600. Orders have flooded in, and employment is now 10 percent higher than it was at its peak in 2001. Other companies in Mexico have made similar transitions.

Some of the country's most promising growth opportunities might arise in unexpected areas. Software engineers at Universidad Nacional Autónoma de México, for example, played an important role in commercializing the Linux operating system through their Gnome project, which opened the door for more possibilities in this arena. And Wal-Mart Stores' acquisition of the food-retailing chain Cifra will provide Mexican suppliers with a global distribution network; Brazilian apparel manufacturers have already used Wal-Mart's reach to establish a global presence.

China's rapid rise as a global exporter seems to have caught some business leaders in middle-income nations by surprise. If they are to create a niche in the global economy, they cannot panic or close their borders; rather, they must restart their reform agenda. If they fail to do so, other more responsive countries will be ready to take their place.

Diana Farrell, Antonio Puron, and Jaana K. Remes,
McKinsey Quarterly, 2005 Number 1.

Notes

1. See the United States Bureau for Labor Statistics unemployment data at http://data.bls.gov.

2. The full research report, *New Horizons: Multinational Company Investment in Developing Economies,* is available at www.mckinsey.com/knowledge/mgi/rp/globalintegration/newhorizons.

3. As part of the Border Industrialization Program, in 1965 the Mexican government authorized the creation of the *maquiladoras* to help boost employment and the overall economy. These foreign-owned assembly plants were allowed to import duty-free machinery and materials temporarily for production or assembly by Mexican labor and then to export the goods, primarily back to the United States. To reduce transport costs, most of the plants were on the Mexico-US border. The benefits and constraints of *maquiladora* operations changed over time, culminating in the elimination of the category in January 2004 as part of NAFTA's final phase of implementation. The government continues to track them separately, however, and the *maquiladora* database is frequently used for economic analyses.

4. See www.dallasfed.org.

5. Diana Farrell, Jaana K. Remes, and Heiner Schulz, "The truth about foreign direct investment in emerging markets," *The McKinsey Quarterly,* 2004 Number 1, pp. 24–35 (www.mckinseyquarterly.com/links/15326).

6. Michal Kwiecinski and Thomas Rüdel, "Poland's investment challenge," *The McKinsey Quarterly,* 2004 Number 3, pp. 19–21 (www.mckinseyquarterly.com/links/15328).

7. On a broader level, the white-goods sector provides an interesting example of NAFTA's impact. Mexico's leading white-goods companies, Acros and Mabe, dominated the protected local market until the 1990s, when they were acquired by Whirlpool and GE, respectively. The Mexican plants were incorporated into the new owners' global production, and as a result this sector's productivity in Mexico rose by 16 percent annually from 1996 to 2001.

8. Ronald C. Ritter and Robert A. Sternfels, "When offshore manufacturing doesn't make sense," *The McKinsey Quarterly*, 2004 Number 4, pp. 124–127 (www.mckinseyquarterly.com/links/15417).

9. Frederick H. Abernathy, John T. Dunlop, Janice H. Hammond, and David Weil, "Globalization in the apparel and textile industries: What is new and what is not?" in Martin Kenney and Richard Florida, *Locating Global Advantage*, Stanford University Press, 2003.

10. Diana Farrell, Jaana K. Remes, and Heiner Schulz, "The truth about foreign direct investment in emerging markets," *The McKinsey Quarterly*, 2004 Number 1, pp. 24–35. (www.mckinseyquarterly .com/links/15326).

11. World Bank, *Doing Business in 2005: Removing Obstacles to Growth*, Oxford University Press, 2005 (www.worldbank.org).

12. Employment data from the Semiconductor Industry Association (SIA) and the US Bureau of Labor Statistics.

13. David Luhnow, "Challenges from China spur Mexican factories to elevate aspirations," *Asian Wall Street Journal*, March 5, 2004.

7

Don't blame trade for US job losses

Martin Neil Baily and Robert Z. Lawrence

IDEAS IN BRIEF

Foreign competition does not account for weak job growth in the United States. From 2000 to 2003, the number of jobs displaced by imports to the United States in fact declined.

Falling exports were a bigger problem for the United States than growing imports. US exports fell by 7.2 percent from 2000 to 2003, while non-US trade grew by 23.5 percent.

The real causes of US job losses were weak domestic demand, rapid productivity growth, and the dollar's strength, which dampened US exports.

The US recession officially ended in late 2001, and ever since, despite recent gains, aggregate job creation has been extremely weak—weaker even than during the "jobless recovery" that followed the 1990–1991 recession (see "Weaker than before"). Contributing most to the overall number of US jobs lost since 2000 has been the manufacturing sector, which shed 2.85 million of them from 2000 to 2003, notwithstanding the relatively mild nature of the recent downturn in the economy as a whole.

Many people in the United States have looked at the enormous US trade deficit and concluded that a flood of imported

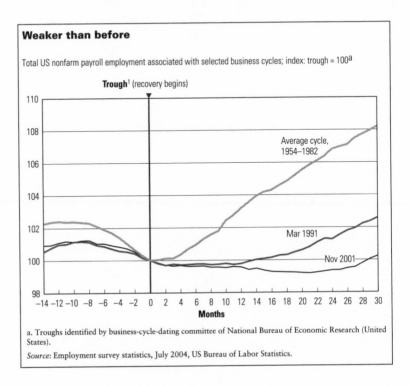

Weaker than before

Total US nonfarm payroll employment associated with selected business cycles; index: trough = 100[a]

a. Troughs identified by business-cycle-dating committee of National Bureau of Economic Research (United States).

Source: Employment survey statistics, July 2004, US Bureau of Labor Statistics.

goods from China and the offshoring of services to India are to blame for the loss of US jobs. CNN's Lou Dobbs has called the problem "a clear call to our business and political leaders that our trade policies simply are not working."[1] The issue isn't the concern solely of US policymakers: the same fears about trade are rampant throughout Europe and Japan, while protectionist sentiment is rising around the world.

But trade, particularly rising imports of goods and services, didn't destroy the vast majority of the jobs lost in the United States since 2000. We analyzed detailed trade and industry data to estimate the extent of job dislocation due to offshoring in the manufacturing and service sectors from 2000 to 2003. This work was the first complete analysis of how the economic downturn, imports, exports, and global competition interact—directly and indirectly—to affect employment.[2]

Our research shows that, in fact, only about 314,000 jobs (11 percent of the manufacturing jobs lost) were lost as a result of trade and that falling exports, not rising imports, were responsible. Service sector offshoring destroyed even fewer jobs. These figures are tiny relative to the millions of positions lost and created every year in the United States by normal market forces.

The real causes of job losses were weak domestic demand, rapid productivity growth, and the dollar's strength, which dampened US exports. It is vital that policymakers understand the forces at work, for otherwise there will be a temptation to apply quick fixes, such as protectionism, that won't restore employment, because they do not address the underlying problems. The real solutions—stimulating domestic demand, cutting the budget deficit, and pushing countries with artificially cheap currencies to let them appreciate against the dollar—are harder to implement but more likely to boost employment.

The decline of manufacturing jobs

Manufacturing's share of total US employment has been falling for at least half a century—a trend that is typical not only of developed economies but also of many developing ones. In the 1990s, manufacturing employment was fairly stable. From 2000 to 2003, however, payroll employment in manufacturing fell by 16.2 percent, the largest decline since the end of World War II[3] and steeper than the declines experienced by other sectors (see "Tough times for US manufacturers").

While the job losses were concentrated among producers of capital goods and apparel, every major manufacturing sector saw payrolls fall. The bursting of the high-tech bubble resulted

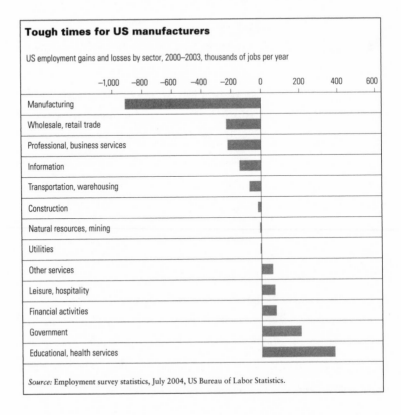

Tough times for US manufacturers

US employment gains and losses by sector, 2000–2003, thousands of jobs per year

	−1,000	−800	−600	−400	−200	0	200	400	600
Manufacturing									
Wholesale, retail trade									
Professional, business services									
Information									
Transportation, warehousing									
Construction									
Natural resources, mining									
Utilities									
Other services									
Leisure, hospitality									
Financial activities									
Government									
Educational, health services									

Source: Employment survey statistics, July 2004, US Bureau of Labor Statistics.

in the loss of half a million jobs in computer and electronics production. Other large declines occurred in machinery, fabricated metal products, and textiles.

For many observers, trade was the obvious culprit. Since 1992 the United States has run an increasingly large trade deficit, which reached $403 billion in 2003. The size of this deficit and its pervasiveness across economic sectors make it tempting to believe that trade played a major role in the manufacturing recession. What these observers have missed is the subtle relationship among productivity growth, domestic demand, exports, and imports. It is this interplay that leads us to the counterintuitive conclusion that the influence of trade has been minor.

The role of trade

During the late 1990s, trade wasn't a significant cause of job losses, because the United States enjoyed full employment. A shortage of labor, not unemployment, was the problem of the day. The trade deficit in part reflected the fact that the country was producing less than it was consuming.

After 2000, as the economy fell into recession, US exports fell. We estimate that more than 3.4 million manufacturing workers were producing goods for export in 2000; by 2003, this number had fallen below 2.7 million. All told, the export slump destroyed 742,000 US manufacturing jobs.

On the import side, though, the picture was very different. It isn't true that manufactured goods flooded into the United States after 2000. In fact, growth in manufactured imports was quite sluggish from 2000 to 2003. And as we will explain, this weakness in imports actually boosted manufacturing employment in 2003 by some 428,000 jobs.

Overall, then, trade accounted for a net loss of no more than 314,000 jobs (a reduction of 742,000 because of weak exports and an increase of 428,000 owing to weak imports), representing only 11 percent of the total manufacturing job loss of 2.85 million. The other 2.54 million jobs disappeared because of the economy's cyclical downturn, which dampened domestic demand for manufactured goods.

The effect of productivity growth

How did imports boost US employment from 2000 to 2003? The answer lies in the rapid growth of productivity in the United States. To understand how this dynamic played out, we will first explore the more intuitive link between productivity and the jobs generated by domestic demand and by exports and then turn to the relationship between productivity and imports. Some economic mechanisms can allow productivity increases to boost output and employment—for example, by making companies and industries more competitive. But from a purely arithmetical standpoint, if productivity (output per employee) is rising, output must increase at least as fast to keep employment from falling. After 2000, domestic US demand grew much less than productivity, so companies needed fewer workers to fill their domestic orders. It was a similar story with exports. They fell sharply in 2001, declined again in 2002, and rose only slightly in 2003. With rising productivity and reduced orders, exporters could meet demand using far fewer employees.

In the case of imports, the impact of productivity is actually reversed because imports displace US jobs rather than create them. The higher the productivity of US industries that compete with imports, the smaller the number of jobs displaced by a given volume of imports. We estimated the number by figuring out how many US workers would have been employed had the same products been made in the United States. When we examined statistics on the productivity of industries that compete with imports, we found that it increased so rapidly from 2000 to 2003 that the number of jobs displaced by imports actually declined.[4]

Although it might seem surprising that net trade played only a small role in the loss of manufacturing jobs after 2000, it actually isn't. Economists often say that international trade acts as an automatic stabilizer in an economy. During a downturn, consumption and investment fall, which mostly affects domestic production and employment; imports, however, are dampened too, and this softens the impact on the domestic economy. International trade might actually have had a positive effect on US employment over this period if not for the fact that US exports were so weak.

Why did exports fall?

Trade's small role in the loss of manufacturing jobs from 2000 to 2003 is a powerful rebuttal to critics of free trade, but that is not the end of our inquiry. Knowing why exports fell is important, since this was the reason for all the job losses associated with trade—albeit only 28 percent of the total decline in manufacturing employment.

Dogs that don't bark

The global growth recession after 2000 and the outright recession in leading markets such as Continental Europe would appear to be the obvious candidates to explain declining US exports. If a slowdown in the global economy were matched by a slowdown in global trade, US exports would weaken even if the United States maintained its share of that trade. To test this hypothesis, consider what actually happened.

According to UN commodity trade data, US exports fell by $46.2 billion, or about 7.2 percent, from 2000 to 2003. Meanwhile, non-US world trade in merchandise *grew* by 23.5 percent. If the ratio between US and non-US trade had remained constant, US exports too would have risen by the same amount. But they didn't, and the question is, why not?

One possible explanation is that US exports might have been concentrated in commodities for which demand was growing relatively slowly. US exports of high-tech goods rose rapidly in the 1990s, for example, but then dropped sharply when the technology sector slumped. Our research shows, however, that this "commodity" effect was quite small—in fact, it helped the United States slightly, boosting its exports by 0.6 percent (about $4 billion). Yes, the United States sells products (such as high-tech gear) that didn't keep pace with the overall rise in world trade. But it also sells goods, such as aircraft (including military aircraft and helicopters), auto parts, automobiles, and medical products, in which world trade grew rapidly. Overall, this commodity effect was nearly a wash.

Another possibility is that demand was weak in countries to which the United States exports—perhaps it was competing in the "wrong" markets. It is indeed true that demand in important US export markets, such as Brazil, Canada, and Europe, was soft. Yet trade with China and Mexico was positive for US exporters. On balance, US export markets grew somewhat more slowly than did total world trade, so this "country" effect does explain a little of the weakness of US exports, but only a little.

Competitiveness and the dollar

Or perhaps US companies simply became less competitive compared with producers in other countries. Loss of competitiveness is a vague term that can reflect a number of factors, including the entry of new competitors such as China and India, an improvement in the quality of foreign goods, or a change in the sourcing patterns of US multinationals away from US goods. Such structural factors, though, have been at work for some time. They therefore seem unlikely to be the main reasons for the rather abrupt shift from rapid export growth in the 1990s to falling exports in 2001 and 2002.

Much of the most important reason US exports became less competitive was the high value of the dollar, which rose from the late 1990s through early 2002, boosted by private capital inflows in the 1990s. Even though the US economy later weakened, these inflows continued after 2000, since foreign investors still hoped to find higher returns in the United States than elsewhere. As time went on, the dollar was propped up more by capital inflows from foreign governments purchasing US Treasuries and other dollar assets. (Prime examples of this trend were Asian countries with currencies pegged to the dollar and countries that bought dollars in an attempt to limit the appreciation of their own currencies as the dollar started to weaken in 2002.) The dollar has now fallen sharply against the euro, but the damage has been done. Experience shows that there is a long lag (about three years) before changes in exchange rates have their full effect on export volumes.

We estimate that if the dollar hadn't increased in value after 2000, exports would have risen by $29.3 billion over the next three years rather than falling by $50.7 billion. Productivity was growing so fast that this export growth wouldn't have halted the loss of manufacturing jobs, but the number lost as a result of the country's export performance would have been 447,000 instead of the 742,000 actually recorded. After adding back the 428,000 jobs related to changes in imports, trade's impact on manufacturing employment would have been practically zero.

In short, the appreciation of the dollar accounts for most of the erosion in the US share of world markets. It is by far the most compelling explanation for the weakness of US exports and, hence, for the number of manufacturing jobs lost to trade.

What role did offshoring play?

The development of India's business-process-outsourcing sector, which is heavily geared toward exports to the United States, has added a new layer of concern about US jobs, particularly good ones. With large numbers of college-educated, English-speaking, highly motivated workers in India, even white-collar workers in the United States feel threatened.[5] But the figures so far suggest that the number of jobs transferred to India is tiny relative to employment in the US service sector. One powerful indicator of this reality is the relative health of employment in computer services during recent years, given the weakness of domestic US demand for technology services.

A drop in the bucket

Adding software and business-process jobs together, about 274,000 jobs,[6] at most, moved to India from 2000 to 2003—equivalent to an annual average change of about 91,500 positions. Although the costs were substantial for the displaced employees, a job shift of this size is small compared with the

2.1 million service jobs created every year during the 1990s and minor compared even with the net annual job increase of about 327,000 from 2000 to 2003.

Employment in IT and IT-enabled occupations has actually been surprisingly strong in the past few years. A look at employment patterns in the IT occupations that offshoring might have affected (see "Small change overall") reveals that total employment in computer-related service occupations dropped only modestly from 1999 to 2003.[7] Moreover, the job decline after 2000 followed a huge technology boom in the late 1990s, culminating in the surge of employment and investment needed to resolve the Y2K problem. The employment levels reached in 2000 were unsustainable regardless of what happened to US trade in services with India.

Winners and losers

While the overall change was small, important shifts did take place in the mix of employment within computer occupations. The biggest losers were computer programmers and computer support personnel. For the latter group, employment surged from 1999 to 2000, strongly suggesting a Y2K effect; employment in 2003 was still above the 1999 level.

For computer programmers, however, the decline of 99,090 jobs probably was the result of offshoring to India. We estimate that as many as 134,000 software-related jobs were created in India to serve the United States—roughly equivalent to the number of US software sector jobs lost. As trade in services with India became cheaper and easier, the computer-programming sector followed the laws of comparative advantage, with basic programming jobs moving to low-wage countries. At the higher end

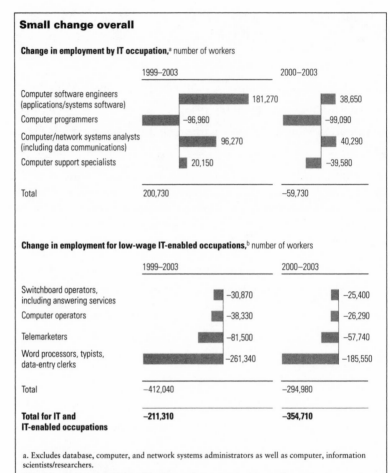

Small change overall

Change in employment by IT occupation,[a] number of workers

	1999–2003	2000–2003
Computer software engineers (applications/systems software)	181,270	38,650
Computer programmers	−96,960	−99,090
Computer/network systems analysts (including data communications)	96,270	40,290
Computer support specialists	20,150	−39,580
Total	200,730	−59,730

Change in employment for low-wage IT-enabled occupations,[b] number of workers

	1999–2003	2000–2003
Switchboard operators, including answering services	−30,870	−25,400
Computer operators	−38,330	−26,290
Telemarketers	−81,500	−57,740
Word processors, typists, data-entry clerks	−261,340	−185,550
Total	−412,040	−294,980
Total for IT and IT-enabled occupations	**−211,310**	**−354,710**

a. Excludes database, computer, and network systems administrators as well as computer, information scientists/researchers.

b. Excludes production workers in IT hardware industry; manufacturing employment in computer, semiconductor industries fell very sharply after 2000.

Source: Occupational employment statistics, US Bureau of Labor.

of the spectrum, though, jobs continued to proliferate in the United States. From 2000 to 2003, the number of US computer software engineers and computer and network systems analysts, who work on higher-end applications and systems, actually increased, thereby offsetting the loss of computer-programming and computer support jobs over the same period.

How to get back on track

Our research focused on understanding the causes of job losses rather than identifying prescriptions to improve the situation. Nevertheless, this work holds a powerful implication for government leaders. Since trade and offshoring weren't the primary reasons for the weak post-2000 US employment performance, they shouldn't be the focus of policies to create or restore jobs. In particular, imports didn't cause the job losses, so there is no case for trade restrictions. Instead, policymakers should attack the real roots of declining employment: weak domestic demand and a dollar-driven decline in exports.

One task should be to stimulate domestic demand, whose weakness helped account for 89 percent of lost manufacturing jobs. Recent expansionary fiscal and monetary policies have been moving the economy in the right direction; now it is a matter of letting them aid the economy's natural recovery. Once it is well established, a sustained effort to reduce the federal budget deficit would help to lower interest rates and reduce the overvaluation of the dollar—and would be good economic policy in any case.

Since the strong dollar was in large part responsible for the falling level of exports and thus for some of the loss of manufacturing jobs, US policymakers should continue to promote exchange rate flexibility on the part of other countries. Asian governments that have been intervening in foreign-exchange markets to prevent their currencies from appreciating against a declining dollar (and therefore from damaging exports to the United States) should be encouraged to let dollar depreciation run its course. The dollar might need to decline further against other currencies, including the euro.

Although stimulating demand and encouraging exchange rate flexibility will address the root causes of US job losses, we recognize that these policies will not restore every lost job or help every displaced worker. The best strategies for dealing with the adverse effects of trade-related job dislocation are trade-adjustment-assistance programs that give workers opportunities to improve their skills.[8] Such initiatives should have the added benefit of helping to defuse protectionist pressures. Defusing them is critical because protectionism isn't merely the wrong answer to US job losses; it is a response to the wrong question.

The authors wish to thank Jacob Kirkegaard and Katharina Plück, of the Institute for International Economics, and Magali Junowicz for their assistance in the preparation of the underlying paper.

Martin Neil Baily and Robert Z. Lawrence,
McKinsey Quarterly, 2005 Number 1.

Notes

1. Lou Dobbs, "A home advantage for US corporations," CNN, August 27, 2004.

2. For the full details of our analysis, see Martin Neil Baily and Robert Z. Lawrence, *What Happened to the Great US Job Machine? The Role of Trade and Offshoring,* a Brookings Paper on Economic Activity published in April 2005.

3. Prior to 2000, the largest decline, from 1979 to 1983, was to 17 million, from 19.4 million—about 12-percent.

4. US manufactured imports rose much more slowly than productivity over these three years. Hence fewer US jobs were displaced by imports in 2003 than in 2000.

5. The literature on the impact of offshoring is extensive. See, for example, Charles L. Schultze, *Offshoring, Import Competition, and the Jobless Recovery,* Brookings Institution Policy Brief Number 136, August 2004 (www.brookings.edu); Lael Brainard and Robert E. Litan, *"Offshoring" Service Jobs: Bane or Boon—and What to Do?* Brookings Institution Policy Brief Number 132, April 2004 (www.brookings.edu); Jagdish Bhagwati, Arvind Panagariya, and T. N. Srinivasan, *The Muddles over Outsourcing,* Washington University at St. Louis Economics Working Paper, International Trade Series, Number 0408004, August 2004 (http://econwpa.wustl.edu); Martin N. Baily and Diana Farrell, *Exploding the Myths about Offshoring,* McKinsey Global Institute, April 2004 (www.mckinsey.com/knowledge/mgi/exploding_myths); and Robert D. Atkinson, *Meeting the Offshoring Challenge,* Progressive Policy Institute, New Economy Policy Brief, July 2004 (www.ppionline.org).

6. This estimate is an upper bound. Roughly 134,000 of the jobs were in software and 140,000 in other business processes.

7. Note that this estimate doesn't include production workers in the IT hardware industry. Manufacturing employment in the computer and semiconductor industries fell very sharply after 2000.

8. Lori Kletzer and Robert E. Litan, "A prescription to relieve worker anxiety," Policy Brief 01-02, Institute for International Economics, Washington, DC, February 2001 (www.iie.org).

8

The hidden dangers of the informal economy

Diana Farrell

IDEAS IN BRIEF

Some policymakers suppose that the gray market creates jobs and relieves social tensions, while some academics believe it will disappear of its own accord. Neither idea stands up to scrutiny.

Informality stifles economic growth and productivity by tying companies into the dynamics of a gray economy. Unfair cost advantages mean informal operations can steal market share from bigger, more productive formal competitors.

Policymakers should address informality by enforcing business regulations across the board, eliminating red tape, and cutting taxes.

t's no secret that some companies operate partially or wholly outside the law by underreporting employment, avoiding taxes, ignoring product quality and safety regulations, infringing copyrights, and even failing to register as legal entities. The problem is particularly acute in developing countries, but it is widespread in some developed nations too. The World Bank estimates that this informal economy[1] generates 40 percent of the GNP of low-income nations and 17 percent of the GNP of high-income ones.[2] In some industries, such as retailing and construction, informality can account for as much as 80 percent of employment.

Policymakers show surprisingly little concern about this phenomenon. In emerging markets, governments frequently view it as a social issue and fail to understand its damaging effect on productivity and economic growth. The informal economy, they believe, creates jobs for unskilled workers and relieves urban employment tensions. Some academics argue that the informal economy will disappear over time as the formal manufacturing and service sectors grow and create more jobs. Well-meaning development experts believe that informal companies themselves will grow and eventually join the formal economy if they are given credit and other types of technical assistance—hence the popular "microcredit" programs of recent years.

Research by the McKinsey Global Institute (MGI) has found these beliefs to be untrue. Rather than getting smaller, the informal economy is growing in many countries. Over the past ten years, MGI has studied informality within a variety of industries in a range of different countries, including Brazil, India, Poland,

Portugal, Russia, and Turkey. MGI found that the substantial cost advantage that informal companies gain by avoiding taxes and regulations more than offsets their low productivity and small scale. Competition is therefore distorted because inefficient informal players stay in business and prevent more productive, formal companies from gaining market share. Any short-term employment benefits of informality are thus greatly outweighed by its long-term negative impact on economic growth and job creation.

Operating in the gray

Informality is among the most seriously misunderstood of all economic issues. Informal companies evade fiscal and regulatory obligations, including value-added taxes, income taxes, labor market obligations (such as social-security taxes and minimum-wage requirements), and product market regulations (including quality standards, copyrights, and intellectual-property laws). Evasion varies by sector and by the nature of the business: informal retailers tend to avoid paying value-added taxes, informal food processors to ignore product quality and health regulations, and informal construction firms to underreport the number of employees and hours worked.

For many people, the informal economy means street vendors and tiny businesses, and it is true that informality is pervasive among small, traditional concerns with low levels of technology, scale, and standardization. But it is hardly unknown among larger, modern enterprises in developing countries (see "More widespread than you think"), where MGI has found informal supermarket chains, auto parts suppliers, consumer electronics assemblers, and even large-scale industrial operations.

More widespread than you would think

	Informal companies	
	Registered	Unregistered
Modern companies use state-of-the-art business practices and have productivity levels 2–3 times higher than traditional companies	Russian steel manufacturer **Unfair advantage:** *Free electricity* Indian software company **Unfair advantage:** *Copyright infringement*	Brazilian midsize supermarket chain, Chinese auto parts supplier **Unfair advantage:** *Tax avoidance*
Traditional companies use business processes and technologies that are several generations behind state-of-the-art practices	Turkish dairy processor **Unfair advantage:** *Partial avoidance of value-added tax (VAT), income tax, social-security obligations, hygiene standards*	Polish street vendor, Portuguese residential builder **Unfair advantage:** *Tax avoidance, use of informal suppliers*

The extent of informality varies from industry to industry. It is greatest in service businesses such as retailing and construction (see "Shades of gray"), in which companies are often small in scale and geographically dispersed, making it easier to avoid detection. Revenues come from individual consumers and are difficult for auditors to verify. Labor costs are a significant share of total expenses, so companies are tempted to underreport employment. In one country, MGI found that construction workers ran away from sites when government inspectors appeared.

For similar reasons, informality in manufacturing industries is more prevalent in labor-intensive sectors such as apparel and food processing than in capital-intensive ones such as automotive assembly, cement, oil, steel, and telecommunications. Even so, some very large industrial and manufacturing companies operate informally. In India and Russia, for instance, local governments force local power companies to provide free energy to some businesses; subsidies such as these allow informal businesses to continue operating.

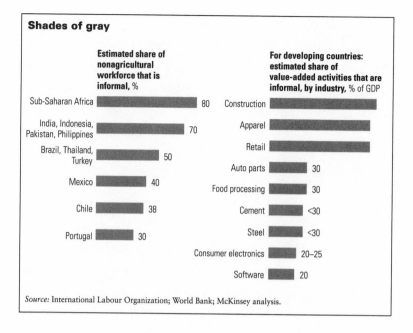

Shades of gray

Estimated share of nonagricultural workforce that is informal, %

Sub-Saharan Africa	80
India, Indonesia, Pakistan, Philippines	70
Brazil, Thailand, Turkey	50
Mexico	40
Chile	38
Portugal	30

For developing countries: estimated share of value-added activities that are informal, by industry, % of GDP

Construction	
Apparel	
Retail	
Auto parts	30
Food processing	30
Cement	<30
Steel	<30
Consumer electronics	20–25
Software	20

Source: International Labour Organization; World Bank; McKinsey analysis.

Three factors contribute to informality. The most obvious is limited enforcement of legal obligations—a result of poorly staffed and organized government enforcement agencies, weak penalties for noncompliance, and ineffective judicial systems. A second factor is the cost of operating formally: red tape, high tax burdens, and costly product quality and worker-safety regulations all prompt businesses to operate in the gray market. Finally, social norms contribute to the problem. In many developing countries, there is little social pressure to comply with the law. In some, many people see evading taxes and regulations as a legitimate way for small businesses to counteract the advantages of large, modern players.

Thus the informal economy is actually growing larger in many places. In Sweden, for instance, it is reported to be on the rise as some companies seek to avoid high taxes and restrictive employment laws. In Brazil, it now employs 50 percent of nonagricultural workers, up from 40 percent a decade ago. Its growth in many emerging markets stems from higher tax burdens and cuts in government enforcement budgets—sometimes the result of fiscal-austerity measures demanded by the International Monetary Fund and other international lenders.

Informality's deleterious effects

Informality stifles economic growth and productivity in two ways. First, the powerful incentives and dynamics that tie companies to the gray economy keep them subscale and unproductive. Second, the cost advantages of avoiding taxes and regulations help informal companies take market share from bigger, more productive formal competitors. Moreover, the adverse consequences of informality aren't solely economic; they are social as well.

The low-productivity trap

Academics, development experts, and government officials often assert that informality will lessen as time goes by and the formal sector grows. MGI research, however, indicates that informal companies become trapped in a self-reinforcing dynamic that confines them to subscale, inefficient, low-productivity work. Around the world, this research shows, they operate at just half the average productivity level of formal companies in the same sectors and at a small fraction of the productivity of the best companies.

Once a business decides to operate informally, its ability to invest in improving its operations and to finance growth declines.

Since many informal companies aren't legal entities, they rarely borrow from formal credit institutions and instead rely on illegal moneylenders that charge exorbitant rates and advance only small amounts. Informal businesses can't rely on the legal system to enforce their contracts, protect property rights, or resolve disputes, so it is risky for them to engage in transactions with parties outside the immediate community. And operating informally creates perverse disincentives for growth, since a larger company might attract more government scrutiny.

Furthermore, informal companies tend to structure their supplier and customer relationships in ways that make it difficult to go aboveboard later; informal retailers, for instance, frequently buy goods from informal producers. Sometimes informal businesses form voluntary associations to enforce contracts and provide financing to members, thereby further deepening the roots of the gray economy. In many countries and industries—for example, the production and distribution of apparel in India, soft drinks in Brazil, and groceries in Russia—entire informal value chains have an almost insurmountable cost advantage over their formal counterparts. In addition, customers of an informal business come to expect very low prices, and many would go elsewhere if it transformed itself into a formal company and had to raise them.

The idea that informal businesses might grow and join the formal economy is therefore a myth. On the contrary, they shun opportunities to modernize and remain trapped in low-productivity operations. There is no better example of this problem than the efforts in the late 1990s of Migros Turk, Turkey's largest grocery retailer, to organize informal grocers under an umbrella brand that would have given them greater purchasing power and operational support. Few joined, for despite the benefits, the plan required them to comply fully with tax and social-security requirements.

Informal players thus persistently drag down a country's overall productivity and standard of living. In Portugal and Turkey, for instance, informality accounts for nearly 50 percent of the overall productivity gap with the United States.

Curbing legitimate companies

Informality also stifles economic growth by preventing larger, more productive formal companies from gaining market share. The cost benefit of avoiding taxes and regulations often amounts to more than 10 percent of the final price. That advantage leaves informal businesses—despite their low productivity—free to undercut their formal competitors and to disrupt the normal competitive process, in which more productive companies capture market share and replace less productive ones.

Across the developing world, formal companies are at a disadvantage. In Russia, informal food retailers gain an estimated 13 percent price advantage over supermarkets by underpaying taxes and buying goods from informal suppliers. MGI found that if these retailers complied with their legal obligations, they would be at a 5 percent price disadvantage to modern supermarkets. Informality thus prevents supermarkets from gaining market share and discourages global retailers from making investments and bringing in new technology and best-practice operating methods.

In Brazil, formal supermarkets have found that they can't profitably acquire informal players, because of the unearned cost advantage. Although supermarkets could increase the productivity of the acquired businesses, their small scale drives net margins to zero once tax obligations are paid (see "Unintended consequences"). Dairy processors in Turkey enjoy informality-related cost savings of almost 20 percent, so these companies survive despite their low productivity. Informal software companies in India appropriate innovations and copyrights without paying for them, reducing the revenues of formal companies. If software piracy rates fell to US levels, the industry's productivity and profitability would soar by nearly 90 percent.

Pervasive informality also slows economic growth by substantially reducing the tax receipts of governments, which must therefore raise the tax rates imposed on formal businesses. In addition to exaggerating the unearned cost advantage of informal ones, higher rates reduce the after-tax earnings that formal companies can invest in productivity-enhancing methods and

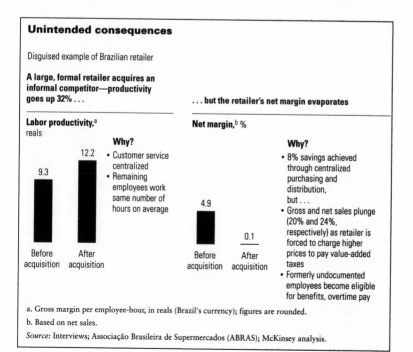

Unintended consequences

Disguised example of Brazilian retailer

A large, formal retailer acquires an informal competitor—productivity goes up 32%...

... but the retailer's net margin evaporates

Labor productivity,[a]
reals

Net margin,[b] %

Why?
- Customer service centralized
- Remaining employees work same number of hours on average

9.3 — Before acquisition
12.2 — After acquisition

Why?
- 8% savings achieved through centralized purchasing and distribution, but...
- Gross and net sales plunge (20% and 24%, respectively) as retailer is forced to charge higher prices to pay value-added taxes
- Formerly undocumented employees become eligible for benefits, overtime pay

4.9 — Before acquisition
0.1 — After acquisition

a. Gross margin per employee-hour, in reals (Brazil's currency); figures are rounded.
b. Based on net sales.

Source: Interviews; Associação Brasileira de Supermercados (ABRAS); McKinsey analysis.

technologies. A vicious cycle may emerge: higher taxes prompt enterprises to operate informally, raising the tax burden on the remaining formal companies, which already pay more than 80 percent of the taxes in most developing nations. This dynamic explains in part why the informal economy is growing in Brazil, notwithstanding a decade of economic liberalization and reform.

The social cost

Society pays too. Most developing countries, considering their stage of economic maturity, have generous social-security plans and labor rules for workers. The problem is that these provisions apply to only a fraction of them: people employed by the public sector and formal companies. The vulnerable workers of the informal economy earn, on average, lower wages, receive poorer health and safety protection, and have less opportunity to unionize.

Moreover, consumers have less choice. In developing countries, they can typically buy either very expensive, high-quality goods and services like those found in rich countries or cheap, low-quality goods and services from informal enterprises—often, without full knowledge of the hazards and risks. Goods and services targeted at the middle market are missing. Consumers may, for example, have a choice only between supersafe pasteurized milk or raw milk, luxurious dwellings or shanties, expensive modern shopping malls or tiny mom-and-pop shops, expensive Western cars or motorcycles and bicycles. The small and midsize businesses that might develop products to meet the needs of middle-market consumers are mostly informal, lacking the ability and incentives to fill the gap.

The mandate for policymakers

Conventional wisdom has it that informality stems from corruption and a lack of government resources, but the experience of MGI suggests otherwise: it has found that governments are insufficiently aware of the huge positive economic and social gains from reducing informality and don't devote enough resources for adequate enforcement of tax and other regulations.

Well-intentioned policymakers may argue that informal companies deserve a break. In a sense that is correct, since it would be impossible and socially damaging to impose a heavy tax and regulatory burden on them. Even when corruption is present, an official social excuse is always offered for their survival: preventing unemployment among workers trapped in obsolete industrial plants with nowhere to go. But closer analysis reveals that in these cases it would be better for the economy and cheaper for the government to compensate laid-off workers with cash benefits and with relocation and retraining packages.

The usual excuses show that governments underestimate what they can and must do to correct all of the sources of informality: high taxes, complex tax systems and regulations, weak enforcement, and social norms. Merely collecting taxes from more companies could well enable a government to cut tax rates without reducing its tax revenue. In Turkey, for instance, MGI found that the state collects just 64 percent of the value-added-tax (VAT) revenue it is owed on retail sales. If it increased enforcement and collected 90 percent, the VAT rate could be lowered to 13 percent (from 18 percent) without decreasing government revenues.

To improve the chances of success and to avoid sudden and massive changes in employment, informality can be addressed one sector at a time. Indeed, no emerging market has ever successfully tightened enforcement of all legal obligations for all sectors simultaneously. The biggest gains come from reducing informality in those where informal players compete directly with formal ones and have a large unearned cost advantage or where increased enforcement has a ripple effect on the rest of the supply chain. In many countries, the collection of retail value-added taxes is a good place to start, since it enables the government to gain information about the revenues of the companies that supply the retailers and therefore improves enforcement among suppliers as well.

Strengthen enforcement

In most countries, the informal economy thrives because of weak enforcement, not regulatory loopholes. The first step, therefore, is to add resources and beef up a government's audit capabilities. Developed countries typically have far more people to collect and enforce taxes than developing ones have (see "Whatever the penalties, enforcement matters"). In addition, developed countries separate tax processing from auditing, and many set up distinct audit units specializing in tax fraud at particular types of companies; Austria and the United Kingdom, for instance, have specialist auditors for large businesses. Many developing countries lack even a separate audit department. And developed countries use sophisticated methods (based, for example, on past reported revenues or on the records of suppliers) to choose companies for audits, but governments in emerging markets investigate companies at random or in reaction to complaints. Ineffective court systems exacerbate the problem by making it difficult to prosecute tax evaders even when they can be identified.

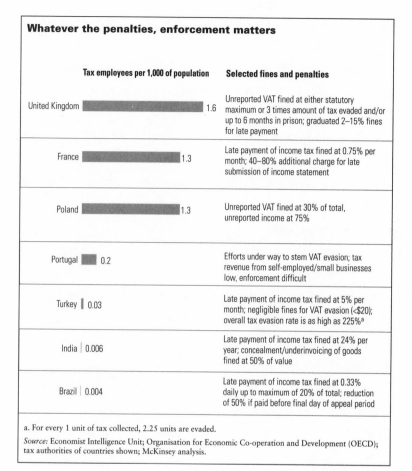

Whatever the penalties, enforcement matters

	Tax employees per 1,000 of population	Selected fines and penalties
United Kingdom	1.6	Unreported VAT fined at either statutory maximum or 3 times amount of tax evaded and/or up to 6 months in prison; graduated 2–15% fines for late payment
France	1.3	Late payment of income tax fined at 0.75% per month; 40–80% additional charge for late submission of income statement
Poland	1.3	Unreported VAT fined at 30% of total, unreported income at 75%
Portugal	0.2	Efforts under way to stem VAT evasion; tax revenue from self-employed/small businesses low, enforcement difficult
Turkey	0.03	Late payment of income tax fined at 5% per month; negligible fines for VAT evasion (<$20); overall tax evasion rate is as high as 225%[a]
India	0.006	Late payment of income tax fined at 24% per year; concealment/underinvoicing of goods fined at 50% of value
Brazil	0.004	Late payment of income tax fined at 0.33% daily up to maximum of 20% of total; reduction of 50% if paid before final day of appeal period

a. For every 1 unit of tax collected, 2.25 units are evaded.

Source: Economist Intelligence Unit; Organisation for Economic Co-operation and Development (OECD); tax authorities of countries shown; McKinsey analysis.

Paradoxically, tax enforcement is also hampered by frequent tax amnesties. Many governments in emerging markets mistakenly believe that they can reduce the level of informality by forgiving past tax debts of companies that come forward. Turkey, for instance, has had ten tax amnesties since 1963—one nearly every four years—and five social-security amnesties since 1983. Their provisions included the right to base the payment of past taxes on historical values of Turkey's currency, the lira. Given the country's high inflation rates, this approach greatly reduces the amount businesses have to pay. Governments forgo significant revenues from such amnesties and, even worse, make ongoing enforcement more difficult, since companies wait for the next amnesty before coming clean.

Governments in emerging markets should not only stop forgiving tax evasion but also increase the penalties for engaging in it. In developed countries, the penalties are usually two to three times the amount of the evaded taxes, coupled with imprisonment if the evasion is persistent or involves more than a set amount. Tax evaders in emerging markets often get by with a slap on the wrist; in Turkey, for instance, the fine for VAT evasion is less than $20.

Another way of improving enforcement is for governments to partner with payments providers such as banks and credit card companies to increase the number of monetary transactions accurately recorded by the collections system and thus to raise the quality of the data available to tax enforcers. Unfortunately, some governments in effect take the opposite approach by levying incremental taxes that discourage the use of debit or credit cards. These governments should instead encourage their use, since the information they provide could improve the collection of value-added taxes.

Eliminate red tape

Streamlining the regulatory burden and reducing red tape also promote enforcement. Registering a new business, for example, is an onerous process in many countries; Hernando de Soto, the noted economist and author, reports that it takes an average of 549 days to register a new bakery in Egypt.[3] When businesses fail to register as legal entities, collecting taxes and enforcing regulations become difficult, if not impossible. Countries with low registration rates must therefore make streamlining and enforcing the rules for registering new businesses a priority. Empowering local governments can help. In Turkey, most businesses—even informal ones—register, mainly because the municipal authorities, starved of resources, are vigilant about collecting the fees. This is a good first step that will make it far easier for the country to improve enforcement.

Simplifying the tax code can also make it easier to enforce. Spain's innovative code for small and midsize businesses varies by sector and relies on their physical characteristics rather than their reported revenue, which is difficult to verify. (Food retailers, for instance, can choose to have their taxes levied on the size of the sales floor.) This option has proved popular, and as a result the government has increased the amount of taxes collected from small and midsize businesses by more than 75 percent.

Cut taxes

Finally, governments in emerging markets must consider reducing and redistributing the tax burden to help slow the growth of informality. Many developing countries have large state sectors and generous social programs similar to those in rich countries. Brazil's government, for instance, spends well over 30 percent of the country's GDP—slightly more than its US counterpart. What's more, in 1913, when the United States had the same per capita income that Brazil has today, the US government spent just 7 percent of the country's GDP. In many developing countries, high debt payments, large military forces, and sizable bureaucracies account for a significant portion of government expenditures.

It may be unrealistic, and even unfair, to expect developing countries to reduce their government spending dramatically. Still, high taxes encumber formal enterprises and are correlated with high levels of informality. Nowhere is this point better illustrated than in the food-retailing industries in Brazil and Mexico. Informal food retailers have captured nearly 80 percent of the market in Brazil, where VAT on food averages 12 percent; social security and income taxes add to the burden. The biggest contributors to the phenomenon of informality are the modern grocery chains, which now command more than 60 percent of the market. In Mexico, by contrast, most food is exempt from VAT. Informality is unknown among modern retailers, and even a substantial number of small, traditional urban retailers register and pay taxes. (Mexico does, however, levy a high VAT on tobacco and alcohol sales, and these sectors consequently suffer from much higher levels of informality.)

Raising collections from currently informal enterprises can help governments cut tax rates. Another way of reducing the tax burden is to redistribute it by shifting some of the burden to personal-income and property taxes. In Brazil, as in other emerging markets, more than 80 percent of all tax revenues are collected from businesses, compared with half that level in developed countries. Raising property and personal-income taxes would not only make it possible to reduce corporate-tax rates but also, perhaps, improve enforcement, since property taxes are typically collected by local governments. Their local roots make it easier for them to ferret out tax evaders, and their limited tax resources give them a strong incentive to do so.

Persistent myths keep developing countries from addressing the informal sector. Yet diminishing its size would, in almost every case, remove barriers to growth and development and generate sizable economic gains. Reducing the level of informality is no easy task and carries risks that are not inconsiderable. But by addressing the root causes of informality—weak enforcement, the high cost of operating formally, and injurious social norms—governments can attack the problem and reduce the possibility of further social disruption.

The author wishes to acknowledge the colleagues around the world who contributed to the McKinsey Global Institute's deep understanding of informality and to the development of this article in one form or another: Didem Dincer Baser, Heinz-Peter Elstrodt, Bill Lewis, David Meen, Vincent Palmade, and Jaana Remes. The perspectives put forth here synthesize a range of past MGI reports, including those on Brazil, India, Poland, Russia, and Turkey, which were developed in close collaboration with each of the local McKinsey offices and with external academic advisers.

Diana Farrell,
McKinsey Quarterly, 2004 Number 3

Notes

1. The informal economy, sometimes called the gray market, refers to companies that are engaged in legitimate business activities but don't fully comply with tax and regulatory obligations—not to outright criminal enterprises, such as drug cartels, mafias, prostitution rings, and illegal gambling operations.

2. Friedrich Schneider, "Size and Measurement of the Informal Economy in 110 Countries around the World," a July 2002 working paper (available at www.worldbank.org).

3. Unpublished working paper, 2003.

9

Reining in Brazil's informal economy

Joe Capp, Heinz-Peter Elstrodt, and William B. Jones, Jr.

IDEAS IN BRIEF

The gray market thrives in Brazil, where the informal economy generates nearly 40 percent of the national income.

Many Brazilian companies ignore regulations and don't pay their taxes, thereby gaining an unfair advantage over their law-abiding counterparts while hurting the nation's productivity.

Brazil's onerous bureaucracy is partly to blame: burdensome regulations, high taxes, and weak enforcement conspire to encourage evasion because the benefits outweigh the relatively small possibility and cost of being caught.

Why are Brazil's economic-growth prospects just 3 to 4 percent a year despite the country's improved monetary and fiscal stability, while fellow emerging giants China and India are increasing their GDPs by 7 to 10 percent? A major but often overlooked reason is Brazil's huge informal economy, which restrains productivity and discourages business investment. This gray market limits the effectiveness of otherwise sound macroeconomic measures and reduces the potential for economic growth. In fact, a study[1] shows that Brazil's economy could grow by an additional 1.5 percent a year if the government emulated the successful efforts of other countries and launched a comprehensive program to fight informality.

The informal economy accounts for about 40 percent of Brazil's gross national income—a much bigger share than it claims in China and India (see "The gray market"). It consists of companies that operate partially or wholly outside the law by avoiding taxes, ignoring product-quality and -safety regulations, infringing copyrights, and sometimes even failing to register as legal entities. In this way, these companies gain a cost advantage and thus compete successfully with their law-abiding counterparts, though on average they achieve only 46 percent of the formal sector's productivity. Formal companies in turn lose out on profits and market share and thus lack the means and incentives to invest in productivity-enhancing measures such as expanding capacity, installing new technologies, and improving the organization. Together, such problems handicap the economic-development process.[2]

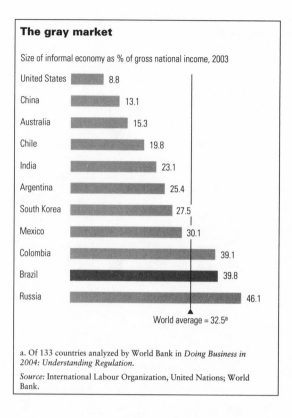

The gray market

Size of informal economy as % of gross national income, 2003

United States	8.8
China	13.1
Australia	15.3
Chile	19.8
India	23.1
Argentina	25.4
South Korea	27.5
Mexico	30.1
Colombia	39.1
Brazil	39.8
Russia	46.1

World average = 32.5[a]

a. Of 133 countries analyzed by World Bank in *Doing Business in 2004: Understanding Regulation.*

Source: International Labour Organization, United Nations; World Bank.

If, as we believe, reducing the size of the gray market is a prerequisite for accelerating Brazil's economic growth, it is worrisome that the situation is getting worse. The level of informal employment was virtually unchanged at about 55 percent from 1992 to 2002, even though during that time 7 percent of the overall workforce migrated from agriculture, where the level of informality is very high—about 90 percent. Instead of finding formal jobs in other sectors, these migrants substantially increased levels of informality in manufacturing, construction, and transportation (see "Under the table in Brazil"). According to data on employment in Brazil's largest metropolitan regions, informal jobs accounted for 87 percent of those created from 1992 to 2002.

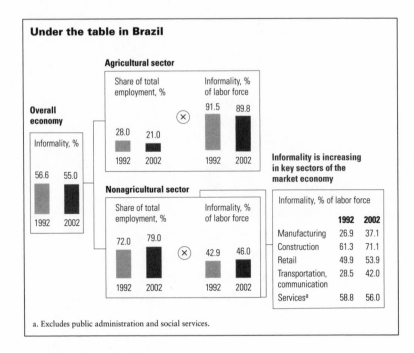

Under the table in Brazil

Overall economy

Informality, %

56.6   55.0

1992   2002

Agricultural sector

Share of total employment, %

28.0   21.0

1992   2002

(×)

Informality, % of labor force

91.5   89.8

1992   2002

Nonagricultural sector

Share of total employment, %

72.0   79.0

1992   2002

(×)

Informality, % of labor force

42.9   46.0

1992   2002

Informality is increasing in key sectors of the market economy

Informality, % of labor force

	1992	2002
Manufacturing	26.9	37.1
Construction	61.3	71.1
Retail	49.9	53.9
Transportation, communication	28.5	42.0
Services[a]	58.8	56.0

a. Excludes public administration and social services.

A gray area

More than half of the labor force is informal in each of 11 sectors that represent upward of 60 percent of total employment: agriculture and livestock, clothing and accessories, construction, domestic services, furniture, gasoline retailing, hotels and restaurants, personal services (such as beauty treatment, hairdressing, and laundry), recreational and cultural activities, retail and wholesale, and textiles. In contrast, only 17 percent of the labor force works in sectors in which the level of informality is comparable to the 20 percent average in developed countries. Most of these workers, however, are employed in nonmarket sectors such as the government, health services, and education. The lion's share of Brazil's market economy is thus subject to the competitive distortions created by informality.

Levels and forms of informality vary according to the value chain of a given sector, the way it is taxed and regulated, and sector-specific schemes for getting past regulatory or tax-enforcement agents. Indeed, informality is so widespread because of its adaptability to the regulatory, technological, and competitive realities of different economic sectors.

Particularly hard-hit are residential construction and other sectors in which small firms serve individuals, thus making the task of auditors and tax collectors more difficult. Informality also pervades labor-intensive sectors, such as food processing, where the gains of evading payroll-related taxes can be huge. In these kinds of sectors, not only very small companies and individuals but also outwardly respectable modern companies operate informally.

Food retailing is a case in point. It isn't surprising that 95 percent of all street vendors operate outside the law, but we estimate that informal retailers operating midsize supermarkets and minimarkets account for an astonishing 60 percent of Brazil's food-retailing market. Compared with Mexico, for example, Brazil has very powerful incentives for informality: evasion of taxes and social charges can more than triple a Brazilian supermarket's income (see "A slanted playing field"). In the food-processing industry, informal jobs are a smaller share—around 40 percent—but the problem is worsening as informal food processors, wholesalers, and retailers integrate, thereby generating a cost advantage of more than 50 percent over the entire value chain. In the meat and dairy segments, informality accounts for nearly 60 percent of employment. In the meat-processing business, we estimate that more than one-third of all output (by weight) comes from informal producers, many of which ignore regulations for handling animal carcasses and thus risk posing serious health consequences for consumers.

In Brazil's audiovisual and software sector, the main source of rapidly increasing informality is the infringement of copyright law. The market share of illegally copied compact discs is booming: from 5 percent in 1997 to 53 percent in 2002. Slack enforcement may be contributing to the problem. From 1999 to 2001, the public attorney's office filed 6,248 copyright-related lawsuits, but only 17 resulted in convictions.

Unlawful producers have also gained share rapidly in the pharmaceuticals industry, where informality is increasing throughout the value chain, and they now hold about one-third of the total market. Among distributors and retailers, schemes that exploit spreads in tax rates between different states have become common. One trick, which can yield price cuts of more than 10 percent, is to simulate the transport of drugs to states with lower tax rates by registering companies and sales in such states but selling in states with high taxes. In addition, more than 30 percent of the labor force in pharmaceutical retailing works for in-

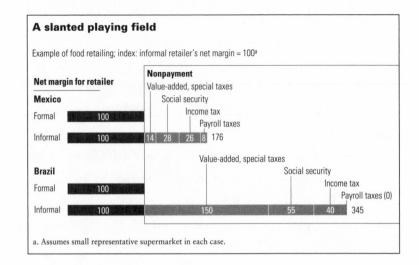

A slanted playing field

Example of food retailing; index: informal retailer's net margin = 100[a]

Net margin for retailer

Nonpayment
Value-added, special taxes
Social security
Income tax
Payroll taxes

Mexico

Formal   100

Informal   100   14   28   26   8   176

Value-added, special taxes
Social security
Income tax
Payroll taxes (0)

Brazil

Formal   100

Informal   100   150   55   40   345

a. Assumes small representative supermarket in each case.

formal employers. The Regional Pharmacy Council of the State of São Paulo[3] has pointed to irregularities in more than half of the pharmacies there, with strong indications of tax evasion in many establishments.

Informality in the gasoline-retailing sector, where at least 20 percent of the workforce is informal, has been increasing rapidly, especially among unaffiliated gas stations, which have raised their market share from 6 percent in 1999 to 27 percent in 2002. Informal players use several methods to evade high gasoline taxes, which amount to almost half of the pump price. At least 10 percent of the volume sold is adulterated (mixed with untaxed industrial solvents, for example), according to a survey by the National Petroleum Agency.[4] A recent congressional investigation, however, found that the practice may be even more widespread. Half of the volume of alcohol fuel sold in Brazil—around 12 percent of the fuel used by the country's passenger cars—is not reported to the tax authorities. Overall tax evasion in the fuel-retailing sector may surpass 3.3 billion reais ($1.2 billion)—an amount greater than all the petroleum royalties that oil producers pay to Brazil's states and municipalities.

The root causes

Although it is important to identify the ways in which informality is practiced, policymakers must also understand the underlying causes to apply an effective remedy. Around the world, informality is driven by three main factors: certain social and demographic trends, the high cost of being formal, and weak law enforcement. Brazil provides a textbook example of each.

Some social and demographic trends, such as the rapid migration to urban centers that is commonplace in developing countries, can generate an excess of unskilled labor, which is drawn to informal employment when the formal economy can't meet the flow. But such trends don't necessarily generate informality unless the cost of adhering to state-imposed legal obligations is high and enforcement is weak. Rigid and complex labor regulations, as well as overregulated capital, product, and land markets, create incentives for companies to operate outside or at the margins of legality. Similar incentives arise from excessive tax burdens. Ultimately, however, companies operate informally when the benefits outweigh the probability and cost of being caught—an equation that looks all the more attractive if legal obligations are not strongly enforced.

Most developing countries have onerous labor regulations, and many also impose excessively rigorous safety and product standards, so only the public sector and big private companies comply with them. A large part of the workforce is thus shifted toward the informal market, which can pay workers more at a lower cost to employers. Comparative studies by the World Bank consistently place Brazil among the countries with the most burdensome regulatory requirements and bureaucracies—for example, opening a business there takes 152 days, three times the global average—and note that Brazil's labor laws rank among the most inflexible in the world.

Another barrier in developing countries is the fiscal regime, meaning both the level of taxes (income, excise, value-added, labor, and social security) and the administrative cost of complying with them. Excessive taxation encourages tax evasion, particularly if an enterprise can thereby cut the final price of a product by 20 to 30 percent. In general, developing countries levy taxes equivalent to 25 percent of GDP, and formal companies pay about 80 percent of all taxes. In comparison, developed countries levy taxes of about 30 percent of GDP, but formal companies pay only half. Like a developed country, Brazil has a high overall tax level, yet its tax system, which is targeted at companies, resembles that of a developing country. The result is one of the world's heaviest corporate tax burdens. According to the International Institute for Management Development (IMD), the overall tax burden in Brazil increased from 26 percent of GDP in 1992 to 36 percent in 2002, and formal companies incurred two-thirds of these taxes.

While the barriers can vary by sector (and either taxes or regulations may predominate), our work shows that informality appears only if institutions and judicial systems are weak, inefficient, or corrupt. Brazil seems to be vulnerable in this respect: it has no specialized commercial courts, few tax collection agents, and relatively lenient penalties for evasion. The problem is compounded by poor transparency and accountability in the different parts of the legal and law-enforcement system—failings that lead to high levels of corruption. A study by Armando Castelar Pinheiro, an economist with Brazil's Institute of Applied Economics Research (IPEA),[5] estimated that a radical improvement in the performance of the Brazilian judiciary would generate a 10.4 percent increase in investment.

By contrast, Asian countries that have joined the ranks of the wealthy nations or dramatically narrowed the gap with them have never had a serious informality problem. Japan, Singapore, South Korea, and Taiwan all benefited from relatively small tax and regulatory burdens as well as from strong legal and law-enforcement systems. So did Western countries in the early stages of their development: the corporate tax burden was only

4 percent of GDP in the United States in 1913, for example, when it had reached Brazil's current stage of economic development. Brazil's corporate tax burden is now nearly 25 percent of GDP.

In Brazil, the drivers of informality are clearly present. This insight is the starting point for action to reduce it and the resulting distortions that impede economic development.

Taking a coordinated approach

Tackling the informal economy can bring significant advances—both in the short term, through sectoral reform, and, when coordinated with structural reform, in the longer term. Now that Brazil's government has restored a degree of macroeconomic stability, efforts to reduce informality should intensify; indeed, given its many underlying causes, powerful vested interests, and creative practitioners, the government must make efforts to tackle it a priority. Such prominent efforts will also help mobilize the business community, policymakers, and society at large. A good model might be Portugal, whose government has identified informality as the most important single cause of the country's productivity gap with leading European nations and launched an economic-development program—Portugal 2010—that gives pride of place to a package of measures for reducing it.[6]

Tailor reform to sectors

Reforms must be adapted to individual sectors. In banking, steel, and telecommunications, relatively few fairly modern companies are seeking competitive advantages through irregular practices. Since informality is already the exception and not the rule, the focus should be on better controls and tax collection processes. But for predominantly informal sectors, such as retailing and residential construction, more structural changes are required. In contrast to Russia, for example, where modern formats face relatively high taxes, Poland launched a program that combined equal taxation for traditional and modern retailers with the allocation of substantial resources to reducing tax evasion. As a result, the country attracted substantial flows of foreign direct investment into the modern retailing sector, which today makes 60 percent of all retail sales in Poland. In Brazil, several government agencies are taking a sectoral view. The federal tax collection agency, for example, now requires leak-measurement devices in all Brazilian beverage plants—a move that could cut 500 million reais from the sector's estimated annual tax evasion of 720 million reais.

Sectoral strategies can often be implemented relatively quickly, without wide-ranging legislative change. They thus provide an opportunity for quick wins that can help sustain political momentum and ensure that public opinion supports deeper structural reforms.

Tackle structural obstacles

Fundamental long-term changes, which hinge on tackling informality's underlying incentives, should accompany sectoral measures that promote short-term progress.

The government of Peru, for example, concluded that large numbers of the poor were in effect excluded from formal economic activity: a complex and extensive bureaucracy made it hard to open businesses legally or to use personal assets in economically efficient ways.[7] This diagnosis led the country to implement a number of measures in the early 1990s to make its economy more formal. Registering a business now takes just a single day instead of 300 and costs $175 rather than $1,200. As a result, 671,000 companies and 558,000 jobs were formalized in Peru from 1991 to 1997.

Spain too introduced structural reforms in the 1990s by simplifying the taxation system and creating a new agency to fight evasion. As a result, the country increased the amount of taxes collected from small companies by more than 75 percent. It also introduced more flexible labor laws, an important move that reduced the costs and risks an employer incurs when registering employees and thus stimulated the creation of formal jobs. These changes contributed to a 40 percent decrease in unemployment in only six years. Among other things, the Spanish reforms allowed employers and employees to negotiate the terms of employment contracts directly rather than having them dictated solely by labor laws. The rules for temporary work—previously frowned upon by legislators—were liberalized, as were the rules for temporary employment agencies. In addition, a new type of permanent job contract was designed for young people and other groups that had unusual difficulty finding positions. The new contract reduced by 60 percent the sum employers must pay workers they lay off. Many barriers to part-time work were removed. More important, the employers' social-security contribution (a percentage of the worker's wage) was cut by 25 to 45 percent for part-time jobs with undefined terms.

Structural reforms are under way in Brazil, where the government has passed public-pension and tax bills and is considering labor market changes. Brazil's congress recently passed legislation modernizing the country's bankruptcy law and is debating measures that, among other things, would reduce social-security charges on low-income salaries and simplify the process of opening a company.

Tighten up the legal system

Since another requirement for the formalization of an economy is an efficient legal system, law reform has been high on the agenda in many countries. Examples of how to make enforcement more efficient abound in both developed and developing economies. The United States and Italy, for instance, impose heavy fines, indexed to the violator's earnings, for tax evasion, and both countries publicize punishment in the media. In addition, the United States has increased the criminal responsibility of accountants in tax evasion cases, and Italy has established fines for auditors who accept products or services without a receipt. In Chile, if a retailer can't prove the origin of its goods they may be confiscated by the tax authorities, and cashiers who don't issue receipts can also be punished.

International experience suggests a need for structures dedicated specifically to mobilizing and coordinating the battle against informality. Ireland, the Netherlands, Spain, and the United States created special agencies to fight the evasion of taxes and social charges; Poland and Spain set up special courts for tax evasion cases. Brazil is debating the creation of an agency to coordinate the efforts of vital government bodies, among them the Public Attorney's Office, the Federal Tax Secretariat, and the Economic Law Secretariat.

Our estimate of an additional 1.5 percent a year of economic growth for Brazil may seem high, but it becomes intuitively more plausible if we recall the benefits of reducing informality.

In a less informal economy, productivity is the main source of competitive advantage, so businesses are encouraged to optimize their processes. Similarly, lower levels of informality reduce distortions in the relative cost of capital and labor, thereby encouraging automation. Reduced informality also promotes consolidation as formal, modern companies—those with greater productivity—gain market share from less productive ones. Finally, a lower level of informality will help increase overall investment, since modern players will understand that they have a fair chance of winning in the competitive fray.

Joe Capp, Heinz-Peter Elstrodt, and William B. Jones Jr.,
McKinsey Quarterly, Web exclusive, January 2005.

Notes

1. The study was undertaken in 2004 by the McKinsey Global Institute (MGI) and McKinsey's office in Sâo Paulo.

2. See Diana Farrell, "The hidden dangers of the informal economy," *The McKinsey Quarterly,* 2004 Number 3, pp. 26–37 (www .mckinseyquarterly.com/links/15990).

3. Conselho Regional de Farmácia do Estado de São Paulo.

4. Agéncia Nacional do Petróleo.

5. Instituto de Pesquisa Econômica Aplicada.

6. Maria Joao Carioca, Rui Diniz, and Bruno Pietracci, "Making Portugal Competitive," *The McKinsey Quarterly,* 2004 Number 3, pp. 60–67 (www.mckinseyquarterly.com/links/16153).

7. The government received support from the nonprofit think tank Institute for Liberty and Democracy (Instituto Libertad y Democracia), based in Lima, Peru. The ILD works with governments to implement institutional reforms that give the poor access to formal property rights for their real-estate holdings and businesses, along with tools to release the capital locked up in those assets.

10

The cost of the gray market in Turkey

Didem Dincer Baser, Diana Farrell, and David E. Meen

IDEAS IN BRIEF

Turkey's informal economy is the largest obstacle to faster and more stable economic growth.

Many companies derive a cost advantage by flouting tax, labor, and product market regulations.

Informality and bureaucracy have hampered foreign direct investment.

Turkey should immediately focus on tax evasion and regulatory enforcement. Better enforcement of sound tax and business regulations will help the government to lower taxes, thereby encouraging more companies to join the formal economy.

n Turkey, as elsewhere, GDP growth depends heavily on the rate of productivity increase. Yet a detailed study by the McKinsey Global Institute (MGI)[1] of 11 sectors of the economy shows that the economy as a whole is performing at little more than half of its potential productivity level.[2] To put the facts another way, Turkish productivity currently stands at just 40 percent of the US level, but we believe that it could reach 70 percent (see "The possible dream").

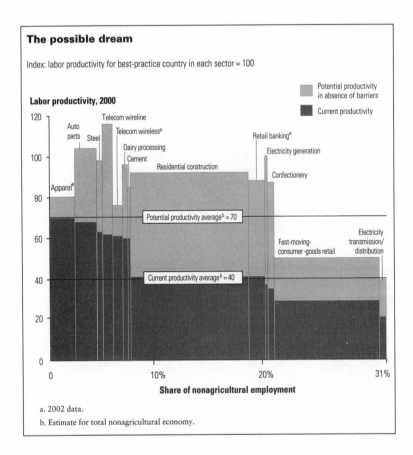

The possible dream

Index: labor productivity for best-practice country in each sector = 100

Potential productivity in absence of barriers

Current productivity

Labor productivity, 2000

Telecom wireline
Auto parts
Steel
Telecom wireless[a]
Dairy processing
Cement
Residential construction
Retail banking[a]
Electricity generation
Confectionery
Apparel[a]

Potential productivity average[b] = 70

Fast-moving-consumer-goods retail
Electricity transmission/distribution

Current productivity average[b] = 40

Share of nonagricultural employment

a. 2002 data.
b. Estimate for total nonagricultural economy.

Thanks to economic reforms set in motion in the 1980s and 1990s, many barriers to productivity evident in other countries we have studied don't exist in Turkey. However, three remaining problems hold back productivity growth: a large informal economy, macroeconomic and political instability, and government ownership. Together, we estimate that these account for 93 percent of the gap between Turkey's current and potential productivity (see "Three fixable problems"). This article concentrates on the causes and effects of Turkey's informal economy, the country's largest obstacle to faster and more stable economic growth.

A two-track economy

Turkey's economy is sharply divided. In every sector, modern companies have adopted cutting-edge technologies, developed

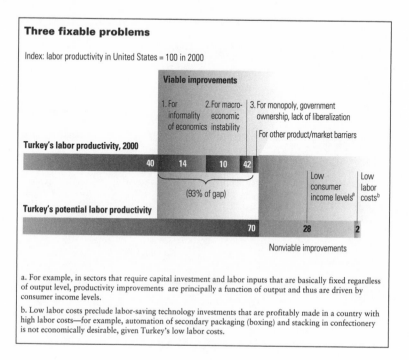

Three fixable problems

Index: labor productivity in United States = 100 in 2000

Viable improvements

1. For informality of economics
2. For macro-economic instability
3. For monopoly, government ownership, lack of liberalization

For other product/market barriers

Turkey's labor productivity, 2000

| 40 | 14 | 10 | 42 |

(93% of gap)

Low consumer income levels[a]

Low labor costs[b]

Turkey's potential labor productivity

| 70 | 28 | 2 |

Nonviable improvements

a. For example, in sectors that require capital investment and labor inputs that are basically fixed regardless of output level, productivity improvements are principally a function of output and thus are driven by consumer income levels.

b. Low labor costs preclude labor-saving technology investments that are profitably made in a country with high labor costs—for example, automation of secondary packaging (boxing) and stacking in confectionery is not economically desirable, given Turkey's low labor costs.

many best-practice operations, and managed to attain real economies of scale. Overall, the average productivity of such modern companies is 62 percent of the US level. However, alongside these effective performers, Turkey has many traditional entities that drag down its overall productivity.[3] They employ half of the labor force in the sectors we studied, and their average productivity is less than a quarter that of the average US enterprise. Traditional companies are typically small or midsize and tend to make relatively poor use of available technologies. Their products and services tend to be of low quality, they have few standardized production processes, and most are hampered by a lack of economies of scale.

The traditional operators' importance to the economy varies. In automotive parts, for example, they represent only 31 percent of all employment, so their drag on the productivity of the sector isn't massive; indeed, the sector's preponderance of efficient companies demonstrates how competitive intensity drives productivity. But in the retailing of fast-moving consumer goods, traditional firms account for 88 percent of all labor. Although this sector's modern players achieve 75 percent of the US productivity level, the average of the sector as a whole is therefore only 29 percent. In telecommunications, electricity generation, and retail banking—all with high capital requirements—traditional operators aren't present at all. "The curse of tradition" shows the extent to which traditional companies drag down productivity in sectors they dominate.

The informal economy impedes productivity improvement

Why don't traditional companies upgrade their operations? The answer lies in the unearned advantages that many gain by remaining in the informal economy.

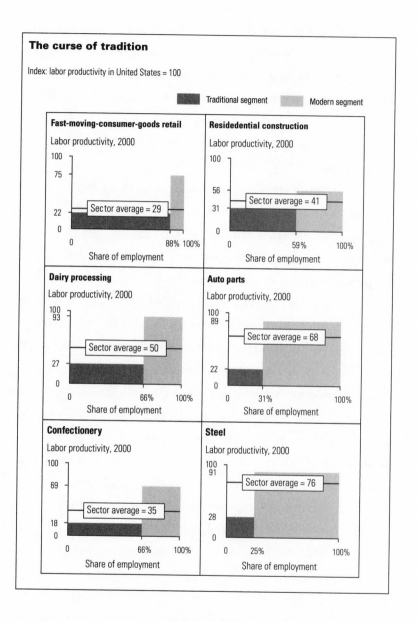

The curse of tradition

Index: labor productivity in United States = 100

■ Traditional segment　　■ Modern segment

Fast-moving-consumer-goods retail
Labor productivity, 2000

Sector average = 29

Share of employment

Residedential construction
Labor productivity, 2000

Sector average = 41

Share of employment

Dairy processing
Labor productivity, 2000

Sector average = 50

Share of employment

Auto parts
Labor productivity, 2000

Sector average = 68

Share of employment

Confectionery
Labor productivity, 2000

Sector average = 35

Share of employment

Steel
Labor productivity, 2000

Sector average = 76

Share of employment

In Turkey as in other emerging economies, traditional companies that have failed to take measures to improve their performance are going out of business in the face of increased
competition from more efficient players. Yet the scale of corporate failure is much more limited than would be expected given

the extent of the operational inefficiency in many sectors. The reason is that so many traditional companies derive a cost advantage by operating informally, that is, by flouting tax, labor, and product market regulations. Several, for example, fail to remit value-added-tax (VAT) or social-security payments, to adhere to hygiene or product quality standards, or to pay minimum wages.

The confectionery sector is a case in point. One manufacturer dominates more than half of the national market, and there is a small foreign presence. But most of the remaining market share is fragmented among 350 companies (see "A crowded field"), 90 percent of them traditional, largely informal operators. As a result, overall productivity in the sector[4] stands at just 35 percent of the US level. The traditional players, with productivity at just 18 percent of US level, suffer from low capacity utilization[5] as well as from low economies of scale in production, a proliferation of products relative to their scale, and low levels of automation. Nevertheless, they avoid being squeezed out of the market by more productive players because evading their income taxes, value-added taxes, and social-security obligations enables the informal players to lower the cost of their products by about 7 percent compared with modern operators. This is just enough, in many cases, to keep them in business.

The size of informal players' unearned cost advantage varies among industries, as does its impact. In the retailing of fast-moving consumer goods, not paying tax remittances could more than double a retailer's monthly income. That isn't enough in the long run to outweigh the overall cost advantage modern retailers enjoy thanks to their superior productivity. However, it is sufficient to enable some companies to survive a few more years even as their turnover erodes. The low productivity of traditional retailers ought to imply a 10 or 20 percent annual decline

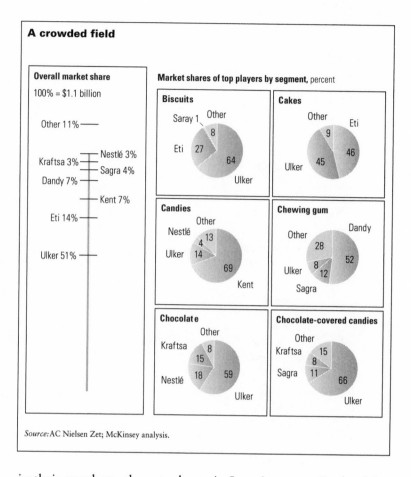

A crowded field

Overall market share
100% = $1.1 billion

Other 11%
Kraftsa 3% — Nestlé 3%
— Sagra 4%
Dandy 7%
— Kent 7%
Eti 14%

Ulker 51%

Market shares of top players by segment, percent

Biscuits
Saray 1, Other
Eti 27
8
64
Ulker

Cakes
Other
Eti
9
46
Ulker 45

Candies
Other
Nestlé
4 13
Ulker 14
69
Kent

Chewing gum
Other
Dandy
28
52
Ulker 8
12
Sagra

Chocolate
Other
Kraftsa
8
15
Nestlé 18 59
Ulker

Chocolate-covered candies
Other
Kraftsa 15
8
Sagra 11
66
Ulker

Source: AC Nielsen Zet; McKinsey analysis.

in their numbers; the actual rate is 5 or 6 percent. In the dairy business, the bankruptcy rate is even lower, with some informal operators enjoying a cost advantage of as much as 20 percent, helping even the most inefficient to stay afloat.

Even in the largely modern automotive parts industry, informal players explain in part why productivity levels are lower than they could be. Turkey is a major player in global markets for car parts, and the industry's total factor productivity stands at 91 percent of the US level.[6] But it could rise still higher—to 127 percent, we estimate, were it not for the informal economy. The modern segment accounts for 69 percent of employment in the automotive parts sector, which outperforms its US counterpart, on average, by 10 percent. But this achievement is still under-mined significantly by small-scale traditional manufacturers that reach only 41 percent of the US productivity level (see "The cost of tradition"). These suppliers use labor to avoid capital invest-ment, produce mostly low-value and low-quality products, and mainly supply the domestic retail market. Many have small op-erations with fewer than 20 employees.

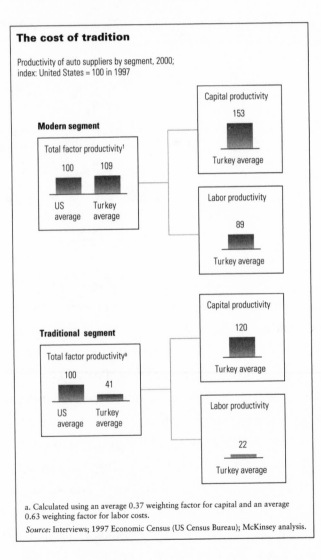

The cost of tradition

Productivity of auto suppliers by segment, 2000; index: United States = 100 in 1997

Modern segment

Total factor productivity[1]

100   109

US average   Turkey average

Capital productivity

153

Turkey average

Labor productivity

89

Turkey average

Traditional segment

Total factor productivity[a]

100   41

US average   Turkey average

Capital productivity

120

Turkey average

Labor productivity

22

Turkey average

a. Calculated using an average 0.37 weighting factor for capital and an average 0.63 weighting factor for labor costs.

Source: Interviews; 1997 Economic Census (US Census Bureau); McKinsey analysis.

Evading taxes and producing substandard parts without penalty permit informal companies to cut their costs by more than 30 percent, which allows them to undercut more modern companies on price. Without such a cost advantage, many would probably go out of business if they failed to raise their productivity. Modern companies would then increase their market share and, hence, the sector's overall productivity.

The substantial cost advantages of the informal economy not only protect traditional firms from going out of business to a significant extent. They also act as a disincentive to improving their productivity. For example, the Bakkalim project attempted by Migros Turk, the country's biggest grocery retailer, involved efforts to organize smaller stores under an umbrella brand that would give them extra purchasing, logistics, and merchandising muscle. Because membership required participants to comply with tax and social-security regulations, few grocers were willing to sign up.

The gray economy deters foreign direct investment

Turkey's level of foreign direct investment is lower in the sectors we studied than the level in many other emerging markets and much lower than one would expect for a country of its size and importance (see "Turkey's investment gap"). Foreign direct investment is crucial not only because of its impact on the input side of the productivity equation but also because foreign companies usually force local ones to be more competitive.

It has been argued that the bureaucracy is to blame for Turkey's low foreign direct investment. Red tape can certainly be onerous; for example, 19 different administrative steps, several of them superfluous in the light of international standard practices, are

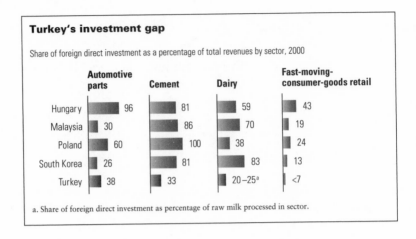

Turkey's investment gap

Share of foreign direct investment as a percentage of total revenues by sector, 2000

	Automotive parts	Cement	Dairy	Fast-moving-consumer-goods retail
Hungary	96	81	59	43
Malaysia	30	86	70	19
Poland	60	100	38	24
South Korea	26	81	83	13
Turkey	38	33	20–25[a]	<7

a. Share of foreign direct investment as percentage of raw milk processed in sector.

required to establish a company. But our interviews suggest that this isn't a fundamental barrier to productivity: it affects all players, foreign and domestic alike, and therefore doesn't distort competitive intensity. Some foreign managers say that certain elements of red tape are just as bad elsewhere, both in developed and developing economies.

Instead, Turkey's poor record on foreign direct investment appears to be due to the same three factors that explain the country's low productivity, including a high level of informal activity, which hampers foreign investors' growth prospects. Nestlé and Danone, for example, both invested in Turkey's dairy market after the liberalization of raw-milk sourcing in the early 1990s, but capacity utilization in the modern producers' plants is almost 30 percent lower than the US average because informal players, with their unearned cost advantages, have clung to a disproportionate share of the market.

Making the economy more formal

Cracking down on informal operators does have a short-term cost: in developing counties, they provide work for large groups of unskilled laborers who migrate to urban centers, and many of these jobs could be lost. But in the long term, higher productivity would create far more jobs. We estimate that 33 percent of the gap between Turkey's current and potential productivity is due to the informal economy.

No doubt, there would be a time lag between job losses and job creation, and the transition wouldn't be easy. Much of the pain could be ameliorated with targeted programs, however, and we contend that tackling the problem of the informal economy will pay very worthwhile long-term dividends.

Since we found no evidence in Turkey of regulatory loopholes that allow companies to avoid tax and other social obligations and to violate product market rules, the first step is to ensure stricter enforcement of existing laws. Poor enforcement is largely the result of weak processes and systems: tax offices are understaffed and poorly organized, for instance, and penalties for evasion negligible. Political decisions exacerbate the problem. Since 1963, Turkey has issued ten tax amnesties, most of which permitted delinquent parties who came forward to pay back taxes in installments and to use old Turkish lira values—a fabulous offer in a country where inflation averaged more than 60 percent a year during the 1990s. Not surprisingly, many people prefer to bide their time until the next tax amnesty rather than make their payments on time.

Bolstering enforcement of a range of regulations across many industries simultaneously would be a massive undertaking. It would be more practical to focus initially on a single area. We believe that this area should be tax evasion, which accounts for the largest portion of the informal operators' cost advantage. For instance, the Turkish government could pressure informal operators in the automotive parts sector to change by preventing evasion of the value-added-tax payments downstream of the suppliers—that is, the evasion of VAT by wholesalers, retailers, and repair shops. Clamping down in this part of the value chain should force compliance throughout the sector.

Better tax enforcement will help the government to lower tax rates, thereby encouraging more companies to join the formal economy. In the retailing of fast-moving consumer goods, for example, the state collects only some 64 percent of the VAT revenue owed. If that could be increased to 90 percent, the VAT rate could be lowered to 13 percent, from 18 percent, with no decrease in state revenues.

Turkey should consider following the lead of Poland, which, under strong pressure from the European Union, began tackling its informal economy in 1993 by focusing on VAT evasion in the retail sector. A combination of comprehensive audits, substantial monetary penalties, and, particularly, a change in cash register requirements to keep better track of sales had a significant impact, according to Polish experts.

If need be, Turkey could narrow its initial effort even further, to the retailing of fast-moving consumer goods. Enforcing VAT has the advantage that compliance by any single company makes enforcement possible both upstream and downstream.[7] The retailing of fast-moving consumer goods is an appropriate sector to choose not only because almost all retail outlets in Turkey are registered and thus easy to identify[8] but also because the product range within this sector is quite broad. As much as 20 percent of total Turkish economic activity is connected with it at some level.

Tougher enforcement of tax and social obligations and of product market regulations is the stick that will encourage traditional companies to join the formal economy and to modernize their operations. A carrot too is needed. Many small and midsize enterprises lack the know-how to modernize, so government and private-enterprise associations ought to educate them. For a start, Turkey should exploit and even try to deepen the assistance the European Union already offers to implement programs (styled after EU models) that help such companies improve their technology, increase their operating efficiency, and access export markets.

Didem Dincer Baser, Diana Farrell, and David E. Meen,
McKinsey Quarterly, 2003 Special Edition: Global directions.

Notes

1. A full version of the study can be found online at www.mckinsey
.com/mgi.

2. The 11 sectors studied were apparel, automotive parts, cement,
confectionery, dairy processing, electricity, residential construction, retail banking, the retailing of fast-moving consumer goods, steel, and
telecommunications. Combined, they account for more than one-quarter
of nonagricultural GDP and more than 30 percent of nonagricultural
employment. They were chosen both to represent the aggregate utilities, services, and manufacturing sectors and because international
benchmarks were available from earlier MGI studies. Unless stated
otherwise, productivity refers to labor productivity.

3. The study revealed two distinct clusters of companies. "Traditional" is the label we gave to those with exceptionally low levels of
productivity. A search for commonalities to explain this phenomenon
revealed one broad characteristic: all traditional companies use business processes and technologies that are at least two, and often three or
four, generations behind current state-of-the-art practices. "Modern"
companies in our study have productivity levels two to three times
higher than those of the traditional companies. Almost invariably,
modern companies use business practices that are much closer to the
state of the art.

4. Labor productivity was used to measure productivity in confectionery, because it is a relatively low-capital sector. Labor productivity
was defined as dollar of value added per labor hour worked. The value
added was adjusted with purchasing power parity (PPP) applied to in-
gredient wholesale prices to measure input and to a market basket of
items to measure output.

5. This problem has plagued the entire sector since the Russian
economy collapsed in 1997, taking with it Turkey's only substantial
export market for confectionery.

6. The auto parts sector comprises more than 1,000 suppliers,

which manufacture different components. Our study measured the productivity of manufacturers of brake systems relative to that of their US counterparts. Total factor productivity measures capital and labor productivity.

7. Businesses remit net VAT payments—that is, the difference between the VAT they receive from their customers and the VAT their suppliers receive from them. Thus, they identify sales from wholesalers, and wholesalers identify sales from manufacturers, which in turn identify raw-material providers.

8. In contrast to tax enforcement, conducted at the state level, the enforcement of the obligation to register businesses (for a relatively small charge) is strict, partly because the responsibility lies with municipalities that want to maximize receipts under their control.

11

Regulation that's good for competition

Scott C. Beardsley and Diana Farrell

IDEAS IN BRIEF

Economic regulation should facilitate fair competition while mitigating the impact of market failures.

Despite good intentions, regulation often has negative consequences. Rules to guarantee good minimum wages, for instance, often limit the creation of jobs for low-skilled workers.

A fact-based approach and a transparent process are essential for optimal regulatory decisions. The control of special-interest groups is also key.

Regulation should protect people rather than jobs, let the market pick winning companies and technologies, and take account of the infrastructure needs of nations—and of the differences among them.

The aim of economic regulation should be the same in all sectors: to facilitate fair competition among players or, where natural monopolies exist, to ensure fair pricing and service levels. Greater competition means stronger productivity growth, which in turn means a faster-growing economy and more wealth to share. Yet governments everywhere struggle to get regulation right.

Why regulate at all? First, market economies can't function properly without rules: property rights (including trademarks and patents that protect innovators) underpin transactions, and antitrust laws safeguard fair competition. The painful transition away from Communism in the former Soviet Union is a particularly vivid example of the need for a basic legal framework. Second, regulation is necessary to mitigate broader market failures in generally competitive industries—for example, to protect consumers from abusive practices, to introduce and maintain safety standards, to protect vulnerable workers, and to control environmental pollution. Moreover, some forms of regulation (such as orphan-drug rules for rare diseases) aim to force or encourage businesses to meet the vital needs of unprofitable customers. Third, regulatory intervention is vital in supporting competition and so promoting the welfare of consumers in their dealings with electricity, telecommunications, and other network industries that tend to monopoly because of huge infrastructure requirements.

Regulation often runs into substantial difficulties, however. For starters, there is no manual for implementing market-supporting regulations. When regulators define rules of competition in areas such as predatory pricing and intellectual property, they must constantly strike a tricky balance. Rules and standards to protect consumers must be sufficient, but not so costly as to discourage innovation and halt progress. Governments are too inclined to frame policy through trial and error, confusing economic goals with political and social ones. Although such experiments often reflect genuine choices about the type of market competition a society wishes to have, pressure from special interests for state intervention may not be benign and may completely undermine the economic rationale for regulation. Thus governments sometimes—and often unintentionally—devise rules that hamper competition and create long-term drags on growth.

The McKinsey Global Institute (MGI) believes that poor regulation is the main factor limiting productivity and growth in economies throughout the world, particularly developing ones. India, for example, could raise its labor productivity by 61 percentage points if it removed harmful rules. Brazil could raise its labor productivity by 43 percentage points (see "The regulation straitjacket"). MGI research on Russia suggests that more effective regulation in that country, principally to ensure fair competition, could raise its structural economic growth rate to as much as 8 percent a year without significant capital investment, which it now struggles to raise despite current high oil prices.

In a recent study of 145 countries, the World Bank[1] found that the administrative cost of complying with regulations is three times higher for businesses in poor countries than for those in rich ones. Yet businesses in poor countries have less than half the protection for property rights. Heavy regulation and weak property rights, moreover, exclude the poor from business. Women, young, and low-skilled workers suffer most.

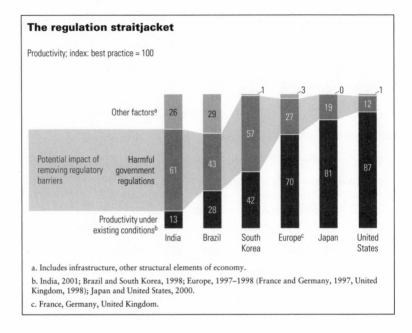

The regulation straitjacket

Productivity; index: best practice = 100

a. Includes infrastructure, other structural elements of economy.

b. India, 2001; Brazil and South Korea, 1998; Europe, 1997–1998 (France and Germany, 1997, United Kingdom, 1998); Japan and United States, 2000.

c. France, Germany, United Kingdom.

Companies in both developing and developed economies are worried. A CEO survey presented at the 2005 World Economic Forum, in Davos, identified overregulation as the most important threat facing businesses. How can governments craft more effective and balanced regulations? MGI studies of 17 economies, as well as McKinsey's long and deep experience working with regulators and businesses, have helped us identify three common regulatory traps and some basic principles to help rule makers avoid them.

Inappropriate regulation of factors of production

Governments sometimes restrict competition in a wide range of sectors by inappropriately regulating markets for factors of production, such as labor and property. They try to prevent abuses and correct market failures, but their efforts frequently have unintended consequences.

Costly labor market regulations

Perversely, regulations that protect jobs often constrain employment. Managers who have only a limited ability to reduce the workforce in a downturn are hesitant to hire new workers. This reluctance makes it harder for competitive companies to grow.

Furthermore, regulations guaranteeing decent wages for the most poorly paid workers often limit the creation of new low-skill jobs in service industries. France, for instance, sets its minimum wage at a level twice that of the United States. As a result, US retailers employ 50 percent more people per capita than do their French counterparts. Although not plum jobs, these do boost the economy's overall ability to create wealth while helping many low-skilled employees avoid social exclusion and giving them an opportunity to move up the income ladder. Instead of raising the minimum wage, with its possibly damaging secondary effects, governments can provide assistance to low-income workers by using earned-income tax credits to reduce their taxes.

Restrictive land and property regulations

Regulating land and property can slow growth by inhibiting capital investment and industrial consolidation. Japan's zoning laws, for example, protect mom-and-pop retail shops but prevent the expansion of more productive large-scale discounters. Small shops account for more than 50 percent of the Japanese retailing sector, compared with less than a quarter in the United States.

Unclear land titles and property rights also stifle growth. In the Philippines, as Hernando de Soto shows in *The Mystery of Capital: Why Capitalism Triumphs in the West and Fails Everywhere Else*,[2] it can take 13 to 25 years and almost 170 steps and signatures to acquire a piece of land legally. As a result, 60 to 70 percent of the country's people don't have legal title to their land. This problem not only precludes the development of a mortgage market and, hence, of a robust financial system but also removes the main source of collateral for small-business owners and entrepreneurs. It is also hard for bigger companies to obtain enough land.

Overregulation of competitive sectors

In most countries that MGI has studied, the biggest constraints on economic growth result from inappropriate and unevenly enforced regulations in naturally competitive manufacturing and service sectors, such as consumer goods and construction.

Protectionist market entry regulations

To protect local industry and employment, governments create barriers such as import tariffs and restrictions on foreign direct investment. But protection of this kind insulates local companies from competition and so removes their incentive to provide better and cheaper goods and services, thereby harming the broader economy.

In India, for example, a small-scale-reservation law designates hundreds of products that only companies below a certain size may manufacture. It also restricts investments in fixed assets by companies that produce most of their output for the domestic market. Both domestic and foreign manufacturers therefore can't reach economies of scale.

Restrictive product market regulations

Governments rightly create safety standards to ensure that electrical appliances are not a fire hazard and food standards to protect the people's health. But some product market regulations make it harder for companies to innovate and become more productive. In the long run, consumers and the whole economy lose out.

Japan's regulations governing the materials and techniques used in home construction, for example, aim to preserve the national character of the country's building stock. They work: every house in Japan looks different from other houses and is uniquely Japanese. But the construction industry can't raise its productivity through standardization, which would make housing cheaper. It would be better if consumers could decide for themselves whether to pay an aesthetic premium.

Germany restricts the hours when retail stores can be open in order to protect their workers and to make Sundays special. But these regulations, combined with high minimum wages and with zoning laws limiting hypermarkets, have helped keep the productivity of German retailing 15 percent below that of retailing in the United States.

Inflexible regulation of former monopoly industries

When governments liberalize utilities, railroads, and other network industries, the potential productivity gains are enormous. Utilities usually account for 10 percent or more of a nation's

GDP, and their prices affect the performance of companies throughout the economy.

To create competition in sectors such as telephony and electricity, regulators often try to lessen the market power of incumbent former monopolists. One common approach involves requiring them to let new retailers use their networks at a favorable wholesale price while still insisting that they provide universal coverage for profitable and unprofitable customers alike. Competition is vibrant in such former monopoly industries of most developed economies. The transfer of profits away from the incumbents has been substantial, and prices have tumbled in some sectors: from 1990 to 2002, for example, the cost of fixed-line telephone calls fell by almost 50 percent in the countries of the Organisation for Economic Co-operation and Development (see "Plummeting"). The granting of licenses to a host of new mobile-telephony operators has also increased competition and demand, improved the infrastructure, and cut prices.

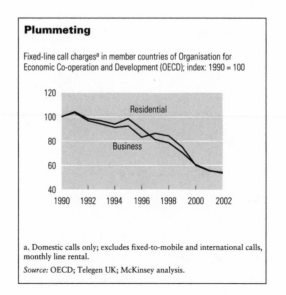

Plummeting

Fixed-line call charges[a] in member countries of Organisation for Economic Co-operation and Development (OECD); index: 1990 = 100

a. Domestic calls only; excludes fixed-to-mobile and international calls, monthly line rental.

Source: OECD; Telegen UK; McKinsey analysis.

Governments, however, often struggle to create flexible frameworks that anticipate and respond to conditions as markets evolve. In telecommunications, for example, regulators in developed markets are struggling to take account of new technologies that, along with existing regulations, are changing the balance of power between incumbents and attackers. Although alternative platforms such as cable, wireless, and VoIP (Voice over Internet Protocol) are substitutes for traditional fixed-line telephony, they tend to be regulated separately and, in some cases, circumvent regulation altogether.

As a result, the challengers are gradually eroding fixed-line telephony, which still generally accounts for a majority of the revenues and profits of the incumbents. Under current cost structures, if such regulatory asymmetries are not adjusted to reflect the new reality they will severely reduce the returns of the incumbents' fixed-line business. That will in turn undermine the incumbents' ability to invest in new infrastructures and technologies (such as a national broadband network) that would benefit consumers and the overall economy in the long term.

Getting regulation right

Regulators should keep certain guidelines in mind as they tackle the difficult task of making their rules more effective.

Make regulation fact based and transparent

A fact-based approach and a transparent process are the keys to making optimal regulatory decisions and controlling special-interest groups. Regulators should understand not only how different options will affect the economics of competition in a sector but also their social and political implications. Detailed modeling and analysis are required to clarify the trade-offs and to judge whether the goals of regulation will be met.

Some governments that formerly failed to undertake this kind of analysis are now changing their ways. Until now, for example, India's government has banned foreign direct investment in the retail sector in the belief that modern formats favor the rich and that greater competition wouldn't drive substantial growth elsewhere in the economy. But having undertaken a microeconomic analysis showing that modern-format discounters offer lower prices and that a competitive retail sector would generate productivity growth in one-third of the total economy, the government may lift the ban.

Making regulatory barriers more transparent—for example, by measuring levels of regulation against international benchmarks— helps a country develop a community of support for regulatory reform and therefore puts pressure on the special interests behind the status quo. A community of this kind often includes academics, international organizations (such as the World Bank and the Asian Development Bank), the global media, influential private foundations, private individuals, and, of course, representatives of the one group likely to benefit most: consumers.

Make regulation dynamic

Dynamic rule making is particularly important in heavily regulated sectors. A regulator should continually assess not only the kinds of rules each of them requires but also, if competition is already established, whether fewer rules might make sense. Like taxes, regulations are hard to remove or reduce, but doing so may be necessary to stimulate growth and innovation.

Regulators can make rules more malleable by adopting a "sunset" clause that requires regular reviews of how well regulations fulfill their purpose and either extends their sunset dates or automatically terminates them at a particular time. The US Civil Aeronautics Board Sunset Act of 1984, for example, ended nearly 40 years of close regulation of airline routes and fares by the CAB. This move led to intense competition and to lower prices that helped consumers and the US economy at large.

Today many regulatory laws are also subject to impact assessments: systematic examinations of the advantages and disadvantages of ways to achieve an objective. Most OECD countries have adopted this approach, but they don't use it to the same extent, and many developing countries don't use it at all. Some governments have also established independent consultative bodies, such as the United Kingdom's Better Regulation Task Force.

Regulate factor markets with care

Reforming the rules covering the factors of production can have a major impact. Because of the complex and sensitive trade-offs between economic and social objectives, however, reform must be handled with great care if it is both to win broad support and create economic value.

Spain achieved both goals in the 1990s, when it introduced more flexible labor laws that helped cut unemployment by 40 percent in only six years. Among other things, the reforms let employers and employees negotiate contracts (rather than having labor laws dictate the terms) and created a new type of permanent contract, which reduced the employers' payouts to laid-off workers by 60 percent, for youths and other groups that have unusual difficulty finding jobs.

Belgium, by contrast, maintains generous early-retirement schemes intended to promote corporate restructuring and to keep the peace with labor. But they have generated huge costs for the government and given the country one of Europe's lowest employment rates. Only one in four Belgians aged 55 to 64 works.[3]

Let the market pick the winners

Regulations governing competitive markets should be neutral in their impact on different players. Leveling the field for new entrants, whether at home or abroad, spurs competition by pressing incumbents to match or surpass their productivity. When governments take this perspective, they avoid the regulatory trap of trying to protect enterprises of every scale, from mom-and-pop stores to national airlines.

Regulators clearly have a role in developing national technological standards. But with rare exceptions, they should avoid favoring one product or technology over another, since doing so often reduces incentives to compete and innovate. Europe's decision to deploy the Global System for Mobile Communications (GSM) and to allow roaming and interoperability across borders was effective because these moves helped mobile technology to penetrate European markets more quickly than it did elsewhere. But European telecom ministries had previously urged (and sometimes forced) operators to buy telecom equipment made in the home country—a decision that drove costs much higher than they would otherwise have been.

Enforce regulations evenly

Allowing some players to gain advantage by disregarding the rules also distorts competition. When regulators fail to tackle the gray (informal) economy, in which companies underreport employment, avoid paying taxes, and ignore product quality and safety regulations, the market can't pick the winning products and services. Companies operating partially or wholly outside the law gain substantial cost advantages, which more than offset their low productivity and small scale and help them stay in business. Larger, more productive, and law-abiding companies therefore can't gain market share—a huge problem in low-income nations, where the informal economy generates an estimated 40 percent of GNP. It is widespread in some developed nations too.[4]

To address the problem, governments must devote enough resources to pay for adequate enforcement of tax and other regulations. Many developing countries in particular will have to improve their tax collection and audit capabilities and to increase penalties for those flouting the law. To avoid massive social repercussions in the transitional stage and to increase the chances of success, governments should address the informal economy one sector at a time.

Protect people, not jobs

When regulators try to save employment in a particular sector, they may succeed for a period, but at the expense of job creation elsewhere in the economy. In the United States, for example, anxiety about losing service jobs to offshore providers is widespread. But MGI research indicates that the US economy as a whole gains sizable benefits from offshoring, through corporate savings, additional exports, repatriated profits, and greater productivity.

Rather than seeking to prevent the loss of jobs eliminated through the search for higher productivity, regulators should focus on cushioning the blow for workers who become unemployed and on easing their transition to new jobs. Such assistance could include retraining programs and company-sponsored insurance to offset lower wages. From 1979 to 1999, however, 69 percent of the US workers who lost their jobs through the offshoring of services found new work within six months, and roughly half moved to higher-value-added activities.[5]

In many Western European countries, regulators should also facilitate the creation of new jobs by making labor and product market rules more flexible so that they don't stifle competition and innovation.

Don't regulate business processes

In naturally competitive and liberalized sectors, businesses should be free to decide how best to meet any standards for the health and safety of their products and for protecting the environment. If governments use restrictive regulations to control the operations, organizational structure, and practices of companies—including the way they satisfy their demand for labor—their ability to innovate in pursuit of greater productivity will suffer.

Consider the 1990 US Clean Air Act amendments, which established a "cap-and-trade" system to reduce sulfur dioxide emissions from coal-powered electricity plants. By setting a cap while giving companies the option of trading their rights, regulators encouraged utilities to explore innovative ways of reducing emissions. Companies had an incentive to cut their emissions costs to levels below the market price for the rights and to sell their excess rights to other companies. The scheme achieved its targets more cheaply than expected: experts predicted that the cost of reducing sulfur dioxide emissions would range from $700 to $1,500 a ton, but the final market price of the rights reflected a cost of only $350.

Tailor regulation to national markets

Regulation must reflect the legal and institutional background of specific countries as well as their stage of economic and infrastructure development; copying foreign regulations is rarely appropriate and can be downright harmful. Although benchmarks help to increase transparency, they must be comparable. Factors such as the cost of capital, labor rates, population density, demand patterns, the competitiveness of the industrial structure, and the stage of liberalization vary widely by country. Benchmarks should thus be tailored to the local environment, since they can drive very different regulatory outcomes.

Many developed economies that moved quickly to privatize telecommunications were acting logically when they based their regulatory regimes on the role of the fixed-line incumbents that then dominated the industry. But in some developing countries (including the Czech Republic, Jordan, Malaysia, and Russia), the incumbents' fixed-line networks already have far fewer users than new mobile networks do. In such cases, mobile may be a much more efficient way to provide universal service. It might be appropriate to regulate both kinds of networks in a similar way to ensure the widespread development of a mobile data infrastructure at generally accessible prices.

Remember the need for infrastructure

Rail and telecom networks, water and gas pipelines, and distribution grids are all capital intensive, with long payback periods. Regulators should consider ways to promote and reward investment in these networks. One way might be to let prices for network access be higher than its actual cost so that incumbents can reinvest in or upgrade networks and new players find it worthwhile to build their own. Another possibility is "ring-fencing" new investments by, say, guaranteeing that a new telephony network investment won't be available to other players for a period of time.

Make natural-monopoly trade-offs explicit

Clearly, some cases will involve natural monopolies (or temporary ones in industries such as pharmaceuticals) as well as many types of rail and power infrastructures. Here regulators should make explicit trade-offs between the tight regulation of pricing and the interests of consumers, on the one hand, and the effects of regulation on employment, investments in infrastructures, business models, innovation, quality, universal service, and the like—elements that competition usually drives—on the other. Rural mail, telephony, and rail service, as well as the pricing of orphan drugs for rare diseases, are just a few such questions. The key is to analyze facts and objectives so that their implications become clear and to make explicit trade-offs among the interests of diverse groups of stakeholders. Issues such as cross-subsidies, the protection of intellectual property, and predatory pricing must constantly be evaluated and addressed in these kinds of environments.

Crafting regulations that encourage rather than hinder competition and growth is increasingly tough at a time of accelerating technological change and economic uncertainty. Politicians are under pressure to protect troubled industries and to safeguard jobs. The work of regulators is ever more complex—which makes it ever more vital that they make wise choices.

Scott C. Beardsley and Diana Farrell,
McKinsey Quarterly, 2005 Number 2

Notes

1. International Finance Corporation and World Bank, *Doing Business in 2005: Removing Obstacles to Growth,* Oxford University Press, September 2005; and World Bank, *World Development Report 2005: A Better Investment Climate for Everyone,* Oxford University Press, September 2004.

2. New York: Basic Books, 2000.

3. *Prospero: A New Momentum to Economic Prosperity in Belgium* (2004) is available at www.mckinsey.com/locations/benelux/work/prospero/index.asp. The work is based on data from established Belgian sources, such as the Federal Planning Bureau, the National Bank of Belgium, and the National Institute of Statistics; from international organizations, including the European Commission and the Organisation for Economic Co-operation and Development (OECD); and from discussions with union leaders, politicians, academics, and top executives at Belgium's private and public institutions.

4. Diana Farrell, "The hidden dangers of the informal economy," *The McKinsey Quarterly,* 2004 Number 3, pp. 26–37 (www.mckinseyquarterly.com/links/17280).

5. Lori G. Kletzer, *Job Loss from Imports: Measuring the Costs,* Institute for International Economics, Washington, DC, September 2001 (www.iie.com).

Index

About the Authors

The *real* new economy

Diana Farrell is the director of the McKinsey Global Institute.

Getting IT spending right this time

Diana Farrell is the director of the McKinsey Global Institute. **Terra Terwilliger** is an alumnus from McKinsey's Silicon Valley office. **Allen P. Webb** is a senior editor at the *McKinsey Quarterly*.

A road map for European economic reform

Martin Neil Baily, a senior fellow at the Institute for International Economics and chair of the President's Council of Economic Advisers under President Clinton, is a senior adviser to the McKinsey Global Institute, and **Diana Farrell** is its director.

Domestic services: the hidden key to growth

Martin Neil Baily, a senior fellow at the Institute for International Economics and chair of the President's Council of Economic Advisers under President Clinton, is a senior adviser to the McKinsey Global Institute. **Diana Farrell** is the director of the McKinsey Global Institute, where **Jaana Remes** is a senior fellow.

Boosting government productivity

Thomas Dohrmann is a principal in McKinsey's Washington, DC, office, and **Lenny Mendonca** is a director in McKinsey's San Francisco office and chairman of the McKinsey Global Institute.

Beyond cheap labor: lessons for developing economies

Diana Farrell is the director of the McKinsey Global Institute, **Antonio Puron** is a director in McKinsey's Mexico City office. **Jaana K. Remes** is a senior fellow at the McKinsey Global Institute.

Don't blame trade for US job losses

Martin Neil Baily, a senior fellow at the Institute for International Economics and chair of the President's Council of Economic Advisers under President Clinton, is a senior adviser to the McKinsey Global Institute. **Robert Z. Lawrence** is Albert L. Williams professor of trade and investment in the John F. Kennedy School of Government, Harvard University, and a senior fellow at the Institute for International Economics.

The hidden dangers of the informal economy

Diana Farrell is the director of the McKinsey Global Institute.

Reining in Brazil's informal economy

Joe Capp is an alumnus from McKinsey's São Paulo office, where **William B. Jones Jr.** is a practice expert and **Heinz-Peter Elstrodt** is a director.

The cost of the gray market in Turkey

Didem Dincer is an alumnus from McKinsey's Istanbul office, where **David Meen** is a director emeritus. **Diana Farrell** is the director of the McKinsey Global Institute.

Regulation that's good for competition

Scott C. Beardsley is a director in McKinsey's Brussels office, and **Diana Farrell** is the director of the McKinsey Global Institute.